CW00819257

YOUR TOWNS & CITIES IN

CAMBRIDGESHIRE

AT WAR 1939–45

Dedicated to fond memories of Cambridge, to my sister Troy Hoskin and my brother Daryl Cooper, who are part of the first post-war generation and who both read for their degrees at Churchill College in Cambridge; to all the people of Cambridgeshire: town, gown, and county, who fought so bravely on all fronts in the Second World War, and especially to those who made the supreme sacrifice, particularly the young RAF pilots and the 'Fen Tigers', for our freedom from tyranny.

'Stands the Church clock at ten to three and is there honey still for tea?'
(Rupert Brook, *Grantchester*, 1912)
There is still honey for tea at ten to three in Grantchester today thanks to the bravery and sacrifices of Cambridgeshire at War 1939–1945.

YOUR TOWNS & CITIES IN WORLD WAR TWO

CAMBRIDGESHIRE

AT WAR 1939–45

GLYNIS COOPER

Pen & Sword

MILITARY

AN IMPRINT OF PEN & SWORD BOOKS LTD.
YORKSHIRE – PHILADELPHIA

First published in Great Britain in 2020 by
Pen & Sword Military
An imprint of
Pen & Sword Books Ltd
Yorkshire – Philadelphia

Copyright © Glynis Cooper, 2020

ISBN 978 1 47387 583 8

The right of Glynis Cooper to be identified as Author of this work has been asserted
by her in accordance with the Copyright, Designs and Patents Act 1988.

A CIP catalogue record for this book is
available from the British Library.

All rights reserved. No part of this book may be reproduced or transmitted in any
form or by any means, electronic or mechanical including photocopying, recording
or by any information storage and retrieval system, without permission from the
Publisher in writing.

Typeset by Aura Technology and Software Services, India
Printed and bound in the UK by TJ International

Pen & Sword Books Limited incorporates the imprints of Atlas, Archaeology,
Aviation, Discovery, Family History, Fiction, History, Maritime, Military, Military
Classics, Politics, Select, Transport, True Crime, Air World, Frontline Publishing,
Leo Cooper, Remember When, Seaforth Publishing, The Praetorian Press,
Wharncliffe Local History, Wharncliffe Transport, Wharncliffe True Crime and
White Owl.

For a complete list of Pen & Sword titles please contact

PEN & SWORD BOOKS LIMITED
47 Church Street, Barnsley, South Yorkshire, S70 2AS, England
E-mail: enquiries@pen-and-sword.co.uk
Website: www.pen-and-sword.co.uk

Or
PEN AND SWORD BOOKS
1950 Lawrence Rd, Havertown, PA 19083, USA
E-mail: Uspen-and-sword@casematepublishers.com
Website: www.penandswordbooks.com

Contents

Acknowledgements

I would like to acknowledge the help and encouragement I have received in writing this book from my sister Troy Hoskin who gave me home cooked meals with lots of alcohol and information; for the patience of family, friends and long-suffering husband; from Celia Tyler at Cambridge Central Library; from Churchill College Archive Dept; from local Cambridge historian Mike Petty, and from the editorial team at Pen & Sword.

Introduction

Cambridgeshire today is a much larger county than it was during the Second World War. *The Penguin Guide to Suffolk and Cambridgeshire*, published post-war in 1949, devoted 125 pages to Suffolk and just 25 pages to Cambridgeshire. The original Cambridgeshire County Council, set up in 1888, covered mostly what is now known as South Cambridgeshire together with some of East Cambridgeshire. The neighbouring county council, set up at the same time, went under the quaint name of 'the liberty of the Isle of Ely'. In 1965 these two councils merged to become known as Cambridgeshire and the Isle of Ely. The Local Government Act of 1972 then merged Cambridgeshire and the Isle of Ely with Huntingdonshire and the Soke of Peterborough.

For the sake of simplicity, the resulting much larger county (virtually doubled in size) was known simply as Cambridgeshire. Therefore, the scope of this book will be limited to the county as it was during the Second World War. It includes Cambridge itself which was the county town (it was not awarded city status until 1951); Soham, Histon, Milton, Swavesey, Burwell, Cottenham, Shelford, Sawston, Linton, Melbourn, Duxford, Waterbeach, Fulbourn, Cherry Hinton, Pampisford, Papworth Everard, Gamlingay, Whittlesford, plus a host of smaller villages and hamlets, as well as the villages and hamlets of the Isle of Ely.

Cambridge was (and still is) a trading and administrative centre, as well as the home of the second oldest university (founded 1209) in Britain, and much of the town's industry was centred around the university, while the main industry of the largely rural county was farming, both arable and pastoral. The annual agricultural Stourbridge Fair, held on Stourbridge Common in Cambridge until its abandonment in 1933, was one of the largest in the world.

The county had its own regiment, the Cambridgeshire Regiment, known colloquially as the Fen Tigers, who fought in both world wars. The Second World War, however, was a very different war from the First World War (Great War) of 1914-18. Aerial combat played a larger part and wrought far more death and destruction on the Home Front than had happened in the First World War. Cambridgeshire, however, fared better than many other places, despite its vulnerability in being closer to German occupied territories on the Continent, partly because it did not have the heavy industries of more northern towns or the strategic importance of London, and partly because Hitler had ordered that Cambridge University should not be bombed. In fact, it was rumoured he had ordered that both Cambridge and Oxford universities should be spared, so that, in return, the RAF would not bomb Heidelberg or Gottingen universities. Whatever the truth, the certainty is that all four of these universities suffered remarkably little bomb damage during the Second World War. There was just a single isolated incident of air raid damage, by a lone German fighter plane, to the writing room and music room of the Cambridge University Union Society building. Steel stacks saved most of the books from destruction. Doubtless, on his return, the unfortunate pilot would have been invited to take '*kafe und küchen*' in a meeting with Hitler that he would never forget.

The flatlands of Cambridgeshire proved to be ideal for the establishment of RAF airfields and their proximity to the East Coast was beneficial for accessing German hinterlands. Second World War aeroplanes had limited fuel capacity and could not fly the same distances as modern fighter aircraft. The geographical position of Cambridgeshire made the county very vulnerable to attack from the air and the geography also played a part in the area hosting large numbers of refugees and evacuees throughout the war. There were refugees from Nazi Germany and Hitler's racial and eugenics policies, the children of the *Kindertransport* project – a humanitarian effort prior to the war which rescued around 10,000 predominantly Jewish children – plus evacuees from large cities, northern and coastal towns and the Channel Islands, all places vulnerable to the Luftwaffe and a Nazi invasion.

Background

The twenty years between the end of the First World War and the start of the Second World War had been difficult ones. There was 'no land fit for heroes' when the exhausted troops had returned from the trenches in 1918/1919; just austerity, unemployment, lack of housing, educational and medical facilities. These were followed by the General Strike of 1926, the Wall Street Crash of 1929 and the Great Depression of the 1930s. However, the working classes, who had been so liberally sacrificed in the First World War, had succeeded in gaining social and political reforms in the decades before the war which had also seen the formation of trades unions and the foundation of the Labour Party. As a result of their efforts in the First World War many women won the right to vote and this was followed by the universal franchise of 1928. By this time the Labour Party had gained a considerable following among the working classes who were now keen to gain a fair share of the capitalist cake for which they had worked and struggled for so long. This did not suit an entitled and elite establishment who saw 'the peasants as getting above themselves' and who felt that their aims were influenced by the Communist ideals of the Russian Revolution in 1917/1918.

Communism rapidly became a dirty word and the British Fascist Party was founded in 1923 to uphold traditional ideals mostly popular within the extreme right wing of the Conservative Party. Labour Party members were also tarred with the same brush as Communism and the whole left wing was abhorred by the Fascists. As Lionel Hurst, a leading Fascist party official put it in 1927, *'a Socialist is the most vile specimen of humanity that has ever been seen...'*

Into this mix came Sir Oswald Mosley, a good-looking charismatic man who possessed a gift for oratory. During the 1920s he was a Fabian socialist and Labour MP for Smethwick. He attended a meeting at Cambridge Guildhall in May 1927 where he was loudly heckled by the fascists who wished to prevent him from speaking. During a lull he shouted *'I am not taking my orders from either Moscow or Rome but from the British working class...'* However, disappointed at losing the Ashton-under-Lyne by-election in 1931, Mosley moved fairly rapidly towards the right and in 1932 he founded the British Union of Fascists. Two of Mosley's contemporaries, Arnold Leese and Henry Hamilton Beamish, held strongly anti-Semitic views and were obsessed with the supposed levels of Jewish influence, money and power. Arnold Leese did not like Mosley, believing him to be *'a fake fascist'* who would not endorse the more extreme viewpoints, although Mosley's wife, Diana Mitford, had strong links with the German High Command. She and Mosley were married at the home of Joseph Goebbels, the Reich Minister of Propaganda, in Berlin, with Adolph Hitler as guest of honour.

There was quite a lot of fascist sympathy in Britain during the 1920s and 1930s, mostly a knee-jerk reaction towards Communism and the concept of having to share all things equally, and it was a hotly debated subject, particularly within the University of Cambridge. In the meantime, Hitler had slithered to power through a loophole in the Weimar Constitution and the Nuremburg rallies were gaining notoriety. The increase in the popularity of fascism was becoming increasingly concerning, especially to young students at Cambridge University. Although privileged themselves, many were worried about the effects that fascism would have on democracy and freedom. Out of this uncertainty the 'Cambridge spy-ring' was born sometime during the 1930s. Five young men, all graduates of Cambridge University, who all felt that only Russia was powerful enough to stand up to the forces of fascism, agreed to work for the KGB in secret, believing that was the only way to really protect democracy.

By the time the Second World War started Donald McLean was working in the Foreign Office, Guy Burgess had gone into politics, Anthony Blunt was an MI5 officer, John Cairncross was a civil servant and Kim Philby worked in the Secret Intelligence Service (MI6).

Refugees and the World at War Again

Hitler's hatred of the Jews had become obvious a few years before the outbreak of the Second World War and since 1933 Cambridge had had contact with refugees fleeing from what was fast becoming the Nazi tyranny. The International Aid Committee, incorporated with the International Aid Committee for Children and the Movement for the Care of Children from Germany, and allied to Save the Children, began to rescue children from Europe whose parents were suffering discrimination and penalties on the grounds of their politics, race, religion, physical or mental infirmity. There were various refugee associations around the country but, because of its proximity to London, Cambridge was a popular destination. Requests to find English homes for 'named' children (who would have independent funding from their families) flowed into the offices of the Cambridge Refugee Children's Committee. Initially, however, the committee had not dealt with many Jewish children because, from 1936-1938, it had been mainly occupied with what were termed 'the orphans of the storm'. These were the young refugees from the Spanish Civil War. It was a brutal war and the victorious fascists, led by General Franco, were completely ruthless towards those who opposed the Franco regime. Over a million Spaniards 'disappeared', a tragedy of appalling dimensions which has still not been fully resolved by the Spanish government.

A number of young English people had joined the fight against Franco and tales of their experiences began a decline in the enthusiasm hitherto shown for fascism in Britain. The children who escaped were politically aware and fully conscious of the difference between Socialists and National Socialists. Numbers of them had arrived in Cambridge, traumatised, frightened, grieving for their lost families and suffering from violent nightmares. Appeals made to care for, educate and maintain these children were met with generous donations and many of them were initially cared for by three Spanish ladies at Pampisford Vicarage opposite Pampisford School.

Although careful emphasis was laid on a 'Spanish education', the children experienced some difficulties with their new country. There was, of course, the

Basque refugee children group 1937.

language, and certain customs which many of the children found difficult. For example, many of the young Spanish girls objected to the Spanish boys being expected to do 'chores' because this simply did not happen at home in Spain. The Spanish children also nicknamed tea 'coffee cinders' because 'it was so black', which may have been an effect of milk rationing, and, even today, in parts of Spain if tea is served with milk, the milk, and plenty of it, is put into the teapot. The Spanish children did not like the green vegetables either, which had been planted in the vicarage garden and were intended to form a staple part of their diet. Ironically, the day the children left the vicarage to live in Salisbury Villas (a house owned by Jesus College) on Station Road in Cambridge, as one of the children put it, *'heaven sent a goat to eat all the cabbages!'*

However, *Kristallnacht*, the night of broken glass, (9-10 November 1938), when Hitler's regime turned viciously on the Jews, proved to be the catalyst for Jewish refugees from Austria, Czechoslovakia and Germany. A major problem was that adult Jewish people were perceived as a threat, and therefore dangerous, by many western European countries who refused to take Jewish refugees. Britain, however, despite some considerable anti-Jewish feeling, did agree to take a number of

Pampisford Vicarage where Basque refugee children from the Spanish Civil War found shelter in 1937.

unaccompanied Jewish children. After the annexation of Czechoslovakia, Marie Schmolka, a Jewish lady from Prague, wrote to foreign ambassadors appealing for help, initially on behalf of Czechoslovak refugees. Doreen Warriner, a representative of the British Committee for Refugees from Czechoslovakia, responded, and the idea of the *Kindertransport* was born. Sir Nicholas Winton was charged with much of the set-up and organisation of the scheme. Two hundred and fifty Czech refugees arrived from Prague and these were followed by more from the Sudetenland as Hitler began his annexation of territories. It was now estimated that there were over 60,000 potential child refugees, but the British Government had decided that only limited numbers could be allowed. Between May 1936 and June 1937 just 124 children had arrived as refugees, followed by a further 377 mostly Spanish children between June 1937 and November 1938. Cambridge, until this point, had been more concerned with children escaping from Spanish Civil War atrocities, but, after *Kristallnacht*, the city quickly realised that Jewish child refugees had to become a top priority if they were to escape Hitler's deadly intentions. The Cambridge Refugee Committee had its headquarters at 55 Hills Road in the city, close to the railway station. The same building housed the committee and regional offices of the Refugee Children's Movement and was also the headquarters of the East Anglian Regional Council for Refugees. The bulk of the work was done by volunteers from both the university and the town, but J.B. Skemp, of Gonville and Caius College, was appointed as salaried assistant secretary and warden of the '55 Club' for refugees. The club had a canteen, reading room (which provided books in English, French and German), games room, lecture room and a music room. In addition, there was a hostel for refugee children on Grange Road in Cambridge.

Getting children at risk out of Germany, Austria and Czechoslovakia became an absolute priority, and, despite some government reluctance, it was agreed that an initial target should be set to rescue 10,000 children and bring them to England as soon as possible. The *Kindertransport*, which operated by transporting children across Europe by train, mainly from the central rail points of Berlin or Vienna, to the Channel ports, was of vital importance. The most favoured sea route was from the Hook of Holland to the East Anglian port of Harwich and from Harwich to London by train. Once in London, the children's details would be processed and then many were sent by train to Cambridge. To commemorate this fact a monument to the *Kindertransport* has been placed on Hope Square outside Liverpool Street in London (near the 'MacDonald's' entrance), which was then the main railway station for Cambridge. The 2006 bronze sculpture (by Frank Meisher Arie Ovadron) shows five children (two boys and three girls) with their luggage and each wearing expressions of a curious vulnerability. Around the sides of its base are displayed the names of the towns and cities from which the children came: Danzig, Breslau, Prague, Hamburg, Mannheim, Leipzig, Vienna, Cologne, Hanover, Nuremburg, Stuttgart, Dusseldorf, Frankfurt, Bremen and Munich.

Under this new scheme the first *Kindertransport* left Berlin on 1 December 1938, arriving in Harwich the following day with 196 children on board from a Jewish orphanage which had been attacked during *Kristallnacht*; but the first one from Vienna did not leave until 10 December. Some of the transports carried only about 30 or 40 children on board; others carried up to 500. In some cases, whole orphanages and schools travelled across Europe to safety in this manner. Much of the organisation was done from 55 Hills Road but, by early 1939, there were so many administrative duties and telephone expenses involved that a dedicated office was opened in the adjoining property, 53 Hills Road. It was from this unremarkable pair of semi-detached houses just down the road from Cambridge railway station that one of the most ambitious and successful rescues of vulnerable children from the clutches of the Nazis was carried out.

Memorial to the children of the Kindertransport 1938 on Hope Square at Liverpool Street Station in London.

53-55 Hills Road home of the 55 Club of the charitable organisation which organised the Kindertransport in 1938.

Initially, it was never intended that the children would not return home after the war and they were classified into three main groups: Jews, Zionists, non-Aryan Christians. This was in readiness for eventual repatriation to their homelands and their families. Only when the full extent of the Holocaust became known after the war had ended did it become obvious that many of these children had no home and no family left. They were alone in a world from which most of their compatriots had been eliminated. Children whose expenses and upkeep had been guaranteed by family and friends, or other individuals, left the ports for London after identity checks and medical checks. Although he was no relation, one Jewish boy, now a man in his early nineties, was sponsored by the future Labour Prime Minister, Clement Attlee, and other British families followed Attlee's example. Children who did not have any financial guarantees for their welfare, were sent to reception camps housed in holiday camps on the East Coast, at Dovercourt (near Harwich) and Pakefield (near Lowestoft), on arrival in England. By the time war was declared on 3 September 9,354 children had been brought to England via the *Kindertransport*. It was a comparatively small number compared to the hundreds of thousands of children who died in the concentration camps, but every child's life saved was a small victory.

The unbearably tragic sight of hundreds of pairs of little boots and shoes taken from the tiniest victims at Auschwitz before they were sent to the gas chambers bears witness to the fate awaiting those who could not escape. On the day war was declared several transports, including one carrying 180 children from Prague, were stopped. Those children could not escape and many of them

Evacuees arriving at Cambridge station from London, 1939. (Courtesy of Cambridge Local Studies)

did not survive the war. Many refugees have said that one of their most vivid childhood memories was of their parents crying bitterly while urging their children to board the trains to freedom. There was certainly some anti-Semitic feeling in Britain greatly fostered by Oswald Mosley's 'blackshirts' and his very vocal henchman, William Joyce, who was later to become Lord Haw-Haw after defecting to the Nazis.

Cambridge was noted for its liberal thinking and humanitarian efforts, but, despite this, there were still misgivings about giving sanctuary to so many children of an enemy power, even if that enemy detested them and did not want them. Once war was declared, all adult German Jews over the age of 16 were treated as aliens and Churchill ordered that they be sent to internment camps. The *Kindertransport* had brought German, Austrian and Czech children to safety whose ages ranged from a few months to 17 years of age, so those German children over 16 years old were also interned and, as a result, 281 of them from Cambridge were interned on the Isle of Man for the duration of the war. The Isle of Man, a pretty island set in the Irish Sea, was sufficiently removed from hostilities so that those interned there did not have too bad a time. Few people could harden their hearts against the remaining sad and bewildered children who had found themselves in a foreign country without their parents or their families in the middle of a war in which one side hated them so much that they believed total extermination was the only answer. However, despite their sadness, the Jewish children were grateful to be safe and most were keen to integrate with their new country. In any case it was not thought that this would be a permanent situation. Indeed, many regarded it as an adventure, never dreaming of the tragedy which lay in wait for them. These children firmly believed that, after the cessation of hostilities, they would all return home to be reunited with their families. Even the authorities, who had grouped them according to their country of origin so that arrangements for repatriation could be made when the time came, shared this belief. The awful truth would not dawn on anyone until the war was finally over and the Allied forces had made their shocking and gruesome discoveries of Hitler's 'death camps'.

The temptation here is to include some individual stories of successful escapes via the *Kindertransport* but, due to the unfortunate recurrence of anti-Semitism and the continuing rise of extreme right-wing groups within the United Kingdom (as of 2018), the author decided that, despite a few already publicised stories, anonymity for those who escaped, and for their descendants, an anonymity which many have gone to great trouble to preserve, was important, and that it was in the best interests of all concerned to give no further details.

War is Declared

The annexation of the Sudetenland had taken place in October 1938, which had been followed by the *Kristallnacht* attacks on German Jews in November 1938 and the invasion of Czech provinces in March 1939. Warning bells were by now ringing loudly in Britain and on 3 June the Military Training Act came into force requiring all men aged 20-21 to be liable for call-up to serve as 'militia men' for a minimum period of four years. It was the first peace-time draft for the country. The final straw was the German invasion of Poland on 1 September 1939. Two days later, when Britain and France finally declared war on Germany, the overall mood of the British people was of resignation rather than surprise. Neville Chamberlain spoke to the nation in a radio broadcast from the Cabinet Room at 10 Downing Street. He explained that the British ambassador in Berlin had handed the German government a note stating that, unless the Germans gave notice by 11am on 3 September that they were prepared to withdraw their troops from Poland, Britain and Germany would be at war. Then came the news that everyone had dreaded.

'*I have to tell you now*,' said Chamberlain in low sombre tones, '*that no such undertaking has been received and that consequently this country is at war with Germany.*'

It was certainly not the outcome that the government had wanted, but it was the one they had feared and expected, despite all Chamberlain's desperate attempts at the Munich talks of September 1938 to secure '*peace in our time*'. That same day the National Service (Armed Forces) Act was passed, declaring that all men aged between 18 and 41 were liable for conscription, followed by the passing of the National Registration Act on 7 September which introduced compulsory identity cards.

The Cambridge Regiment was on full alert and a second battalion was formed in 1939. Initially the regiment served on the Norfolk coast, but then had the misfortune to be sent to the Far East, fighting in Malaya and Singapore. Mothers all over the country felt grief and foreboding as their sons marched off to war. Hadn't they been assured that the Great War had been 'the war to end all wars'? Many had lost husbands, fathers and brothers. Now, just twenty years later, they were being asked to sacrifice their children as well. Cambridgeshire mothers, like mothers all over the country, bit their tongues and told themselves it really was all for the best. This war would not be prolonged and bloody like the last war and Hitler had to be taught a short sharp lesson. They just had to be brave, supportive and cheerful, but secretly many cried into their pillows every night and prayed that if there were casualties it would not be their own much-loved sons.

The first radio broadcasts of news, sport and entertainment had been made in 1920, just after the First World War, and many people now had radios in their own homes. Cambridgeshire folk, like everyone else, had listened with heavy hearts to the declaration of war with Germany. Twenty minutes after the initial announcement of war by Neville Chamberlain air raid sirens had sounded in London although there was no immediate threat of aerial attack from the Germans. Radio had become the main method of communication, especially in rural areas, as all television transmission was suspended. Not many people had television in 1939 but, after the declaration of war, it was decided to switch the Alexandra Palace transmitter in London to jamming German aircraft navigation frequencies. Alexandra Palace was the former BBC television headquarters and was known affectionately as the 'Ally Pally'. Television manufacturing facilities were now adapted for making radio and radar equipment. All cinemas were closed in September but soon re-opened as the government recognised the need for some sort of entertainment and escape from everyday problems. They also realised that cinemas could be used to promote their own propaganda and a number of short films and documentaries were made for this purpose. Football was badly affected as well and initially professional football was suspended, but football grounds re-opened later in September, although those watching games were limited to 8,000 spectators.

By late 1939 there were also sizeable numbers of Polish refugees who had fled to Britain. Russia, as well as Germany, invaded Poland in September 1939. Polish territory was roughly divided equally between Russia and Germany under the terms of a secret pact between General von Ribbentrop and Josef Stalin. The Russians did not formally declare war on Poland; rather they already regarded Poland as part of Russian territories and claimed they were simply saving the country from the Nazis. The reality, however, was a great deal of violence towards the terrified Poles from both sides. Hundreds of thousands died or were deported. Those who could escaped, many to Britain. The Second Polish Corps, part of the Polish armed forces, supported the Allies, and, of those who escaped, many were based in East Anglia, being the region nearest to the coast and home to many of the RAF airfields which gave so much support in the Battle of Britain.

Polish flyers also played a considerable part in the Battle of Britain because they had numbers of slightly older, more experienced and seemingly fearless pilots who fought valiantly alongside their RAF counterparts. Initially the Poles suffered language problems, loneliness, and homesickness in a strange country, but many managed to persevere in learning English and English ways. Squadrons 303 and 306 were exclusively Polish and based at RAF Northolt in Middlesex, but later in the war they transferred to RAF Coltishall, close to the Norfolk coast, and RAF Martlesham Heath near the Suffolk coast. As a result, Polish airmen regularly flew in and out of many of the Cambridgeshire RAF bases including Duxford, the USAAF bases and RAF Mepal.

At this point in the war Russia was still officially neutral and only joined the Allies when Hitler broke the secret pact and invaded Russia in June 1941 in Operation Barbarossa. The Russian government offered an amnesty to those Polish citizens who had survived the *gulags* (forced labour camps) to which they had been deported and even more Poles then fled the country.

After war was declared many refugee committees were set up nationally – Cambridge had twelve. By now children evacuated from cities like London and Birmingham had been added to the *Kindertransport* refugees and those from the Spanish Civil War; and, in addition, there were a number of adult and academic refugees as well. Just keeping records of all the children, refugees and evacuees, was a mammoth task.

Basque refugee children, 1937.

Evacuees

Evacuees were different from refugees. Under Operation Pied Piper, British children from large cities like Manchester, London, Birmingham, Liverpool, Sheffield, Coventry etc., East Coast ports and northern industrial towns, were evacuated from their homes and schools to either the countryside or to smaller towns not considered to be so vulnerable to the attentions of German bombers. Sometimes whole schools were evacuated together. The Roneodex Recording System was used for efficiency and clarity. There was a card for each child carrying details of their name, age, address, religion, place of birth, address of parents and basic health, training and re-emigration details for refugees. Record cards were colour-coded along their edges according to various criteria. A supplementary system of larger record cards recorded fuller details, such as insurance against twenty-two different mishaps or illnesses, clothing, holidays, education or training, health, registration of deaths, as well as all issues and responsibilities for the regional committees.

Grants and donations were the main forms of funding for children and these were also recorded. Cambridge/shire took a total of about 3,000 domestic child evacuees from the country's major cities of Manchester, London and Birmingham. A total of 32 children were sent to the south Cambridgshire village of Barrington; a school group from Chelsea went to neighbouring Orwell; Raynes Park County Grammar School camped out in Meldreth; a school from Reading was evacuated to Gamlingay; Eltisley took quite a few children while Ely took both refugees and evacuees.

Being evacuated to the countryside was something of a cultural shock for city children. The fields and open spaces, devoid of buildings, shops, cinemas, transport, and 'things to do', could prove bewildering and disconcerting for those who had never known anything but city streets. Rural evacuees were usually expected to help out on their hosts' farms, small-holdings or allotments, but there were compensations. Fresh eggs, milk, fruit and vegetables were often more freely available than in the towns, and the boys were taught how to snare rabbits for the pot. Children learned how to grow their own food, make their own clothes, think up their own amusements. Many country cottages did not have inside toilets or bathrooms. Baths were taken once a week in a tin bath placed in front of the fire in the kitchen. Toilet facilities were in an outdoor shed, sometimes a chemical toilet but, more often than not, just a large pail. In some Cambridgeshire villages the policy of waste not, want not, shocked a few of the children when they saw pails of human waste material used as manure and spread over the vegetable patches. Two young brothers evacuated to Orwell said they experienced considerable difficulties eating vegetables grown by their host after they had seen him tip the toilet contents over his vegetable garden. Although they knew that horse manure and cow manure were used to enrich the soil and help the vegetables to grow, they nevertheless felt that using their own waste was a step too far.

Around 250 children were sent out into rural Cambridgeshire, but many children remained in the city where there was more room in the large houses and colleges. The whole of Newnham College was also lent as a girls' hostel between 1939–1940. Some of the older refugee children were approaching an age where they could work, although by 1941 some boys were interned for the duration of the war once they reached 16, but the younger ones needed careful assessment. There was the question of abilities and what type of education or training should be provided, as well as difficulties with curriculums and languages spoken. Refugee children spoke a mix of French, Spanish, German, Italian, Czech, Hebrew and Yiddish. The government provided a bewildering array of information on caring for refugee children, and there were booklets on placing, education, training, welfare, aftercare, re-emigration, hostels, accommodation and evacuation.

THE CHILDREN SET OFF TO MARKET. MRS. BIRD LIFTS LITTLE VIVIENNE INTO THE FARM CART THAT IS TAKING THEM INTO THE NEAREST TOWN TO DO THE WEEK'S SHOPPING FOR THEIR MOTHERS

Evacuee children in haycart 1944. (Courtesy of Cambridge Local Studies)

However, there did not seem to be the same array of information on how to deal with British evacuee children. Several children were very homesick and bed-wetting was a problem for a number of host families. Cleanliness and standards of behaviour often differed between evacuees and host families; although not often as extreme as the case of a two-year-old boy, billeted in one Cambridgeshire village, who leaned out of his bedroom window shouting four-letter profanities. Most villages had a billeting officer who would place children with local families, but initial enthusiasm to offer evacuees a home declined a little as a result of some of the practical problems. Nevertheless, many children had a good experience of evacuation and got on well with their host families, although a few were so unhappy they simply ran away. The situation was obviously not ideal.

It was, however, not just children, who were evacuated to the city and university. Bedford College and the LSE were also evacuated to Cambridge. Peterhouse offered to house the LSE and, at the beginning of September, two days before war was officially declared, the Ministry of Works took over the LSE's London premises and the LSE moved to Cambridge and rented Grove Lodge on Trumpington Street to provide lecture facilities, common rooms and a library.

Soham Village College which gave Jewish refugee children accommodation and education.

Gas Masks

Fearing war for some time, and mindful of the horrors of chemical warfare and gas poisoning from the last war, the authorities had been determined to be well prepared in advance for this aspect of war, and by the end of September 1939 some 38 million gas masks had been distributed around the country, although, in the event, they were never needed. People were expected to carry their gas masks with them at all times, and could be punished for not doing so. Anyone losing their gas mask was forced to replace it at their own, not inconsiderable, expense. The masks were enclosed in a small box with straps and strict instructions as to how they should be packed. Masks for babies encompassed most of the child and must have been hot and claustrophobic for the unfortunate infant. Regular public gas mask drills were held in the city, like those on Ramsden Square, but out in the countryside it was much more difficult to organise such drills, and, in any case, there was far less danger from aerial attack.

The development of the gas mask was in response to the appalling deaths and injuries from the chlorine gas which had first been introduced by the Germans during the First World War. The masks were made of black leather and had a sinister appearance like that of a science fiction monster with bug eyes, a large flat nose/mouthpiece containing a filter, and a tube leading from the side. The supreme irony was that some of the filters contained blue asbestos which, it was not realised at that time, was deadly poisonous. An unknown wit in Cambridgeshire at this time penned some amusing couplets on how to identify the different types of gas.

If you get a choking feeling and a smell of musty hay
You can bet your bottom dollar there's phosgene [lung irritant] *on the way.*
But the smell of bleaching powder inevitably will mean
That the enemy you're meeting is a gas called chlorine [lung irritant]
When your eyes begin a-twitching and for tears you cannot see
It's not mother peeling onions, but a dose of C.A.P [type of teargas]
If the smell resembles pear drops you'd better not delay
It's not father sucking toffee, it's that ruddy K.S.K [type of teargas]
If you catch a pungent odour as you're going home to tea
You can safely put your shirt on it, they're using BBC [type of teargas]
DM.DA. and DC [nasal irritants] *emanate the scent of roses*
But, despite their pretty perfume, they aren't good for human noses.
If for garlic or onions you've a cultivated taste
When in war you meet these odours leave the area in haste

Coping with the black out, Cambridge 1939. (Courtesy of Cambridge Local Studies)

For it's mustard gas, [burning gas] *the hellish stuff, that leaves you one big blister*
And in hospital you'll need the kind attention of Sister
And lastly, while geraniums look pleasant in a bed
Beware this smell in wartime; if it's Lewisite [burning blistering gas] you're dead!

The Blackout

Throughout 1938 'black-out rehearsals' had been held, although black-out regulations were not actually imposed until 1 September 1939, two days before the official declaration of war. Cambridgeshire residents, along with the rest of the country, resigned themselves to the fact that yet again windows and doors had to be covered with dark materials and any light which might help enemy aircraft had to be extinguished. The county was well aware of just how vulnerable it was to German bombers. Street lamps were switched off and the use of torches forbidden; accidents and crime rates rose sharply. To try and reduce accidents it was recommended to wear or carry something white and to look out for red lights of vehicles before stepping off a pavement. The edges of pavements were painted white and people were told to walk slowly on the left-hand side in the dark. White bars were painted on street lamp posts, gates, vehicles and other obstacles. Crime was less easy to tackle as the darkness was on the side of the criminal which made chasing or catching them very difficult. It is difficult to imagine complete night darkness today but on the remoter British islands, where there is scant population and no street lighting, moonless or cloudy nights can be dark to the extent that, without a torch, the only method is to feel your way by shuffling of feet and/or touch. It can be disorientating and scary.

The university initially seemed almost unable to comprehend that war had struck again so soon after the 'war to end all wars'. At King's College, during the early weeks, there was a feeling of considerable confusion and ambiguity. Amateur film shot by a student at St John's College in 1940/1941 shows students walking along 'the backs' laughing and talking, folk punting on the river, tennis tournaments held in the university. A carefree existence reminiscent of Rupert Brooke's poem on Grantchester Vicarage written during the early twentieth century; the lines *'stands the church clock at ten to three and is there honey still for tea…'* were still as pertinent; and there was honey still for tea in the Vicarage gardens over a hundred years after Brooke completed the poem. The students were also notoriously fond of 'pranks' which could be irritating, and, occasionally, even dangerous.

At first, at least 75 per cent of the normal numbers of students were in residence at the university because, at this stage, the government had not decided to call up those under 20 years old. Any spare room or places were filled by students from the University of London colleges and by RAF training units. This meant that, at first, there were no cuts in government grants. Money from unused or unclaimed scholarships, prizes and trust funds was donated to the War Emergency Fund for various purposes. However, the college authorities were not slow to offer help and accommodation when and where needed, especially by the RAF who requisitioned a number of college buildings, and also offered most of the college lawns for use to grow vegetables as a way of promoting the 'Dig for Victory' campaign. King's College, when they had gathered their thoughts together, and not being privy to the unspoken agreement by Hitler that the university should not be attacked, had their stained-glass windows removed in case of aerial bombardment. Corpus Christi, harking back to the medieval past, walled up its college plate in a cellar and hid the college wines in case of invasion. Peterhouse had offered to take in and house the LSE who were evacuating from London. Trinity College remained impassive but offered garden space to grow vegetables for the Dig for Victory campaign and the college was privy to top secret government meetings later in the war.

Corpus Christi College. (Courtesy of Cambridge Local Studies)

Rationing

The man of the moment in this war was Winston Churchill. He had also served in the First World War, in the navy, army and in the government, and he had admired much of David Lloyd George's handling of the situation both at home and abroad, as well as the methods he had used to guide the country through the conflict. Food rationing had been a major issue, although it did not start until 1917, but Churchill recognised that it needed to start at the beginning of this war if stocks and supplies were to be efficiently and effectively conserved and utilised. Cambridgeshire, being a very rural county, took this as seriously as they had during the Great War and folk began, once again, to 'Dig for Victory'.

At the outbreak of war, the Minister of Food, Lord Woolton, had ordered that strict minimal daily rations were to be issued to each adult which consisted of:

1lb (0.5kg) potatoes
1 oz (0.375g) bread
6oz (0.198g) vegetables
2oz (0.036g) oatmeal
1oz (0.018g) fat
½pt (0.25ltr) milk
no meat

Churchill was horrified by the basic Spartan approach of such a diet and ordered Lord Woolton to adopt more generous rations immediately. Churchill was all in favour of food rationing, but he recognised that people needed a basic daily minimum intake of nutrition if they were to work efficiently and make a proper contribution to the war effort. Lord Woolton relented a little; he admitted that there were plenty of supplies of bread, potatoes and vegetables, but warned that meat, cheese, bacon and eggs were in short supply and that they would remain so. The British have always been keen meat eaters, but meat was rationed from the end of September and Lord Woolton was keen to promote a more vegetarian approach. He therefore encouraged the use of vegetarian cookery and developed his own 'Woolton pie' recipe which consisted of carrots, parsnips, potatoes, and turnips in oatmeal, with a potato or pastry crust and served with brown gravy. It was generally unpopular, probably due to the fact that it was rather dry. The addition of a few herbs (which were not rationed), fried onions and the brown gravy within the pie might have made it more palatable.

Bread, although not actually rationed until after the war was over, became one of the most contentious wartime foods. Lord Woolton had insisted that white bread must be replaced with a 'national loaf', a type of brown wholemeal bread which was dismissed as 'mushy and grey' and was fairly universally disliked. The nearest equivalent bread today is a soft wholemeal loaf with oats sprinkled on top. White bread has long been preferred in Britain, but today rye or oat and wholegrain breads are generally regarded as healthier and more nutritious. In Cambridgeshire, many parts of which have a rich black fertile soil, plenty of good natural resources were available and there was also great potential for growing wheat, barley, fruit and vegetables, keeping hens and bees, and obtaining fresh milk from local cows. Children evacuated from the cities marvelled at the rich warm milk they were sometimes given to drink immediately after the cows had been milked. Blackberries, elderberries, wild raspberries and crab apples grew in the hedgerows, while rabbits and birds were often available for the pot.

Petrol rationing was also introduced from 23 September. 'Motor spirit', as petrol was then called, was rationed by coupons allowing so many units per month depending upon the size of the engine. At this time one unit equalled one gallon (just under 4ltrs). Again, this hit Cambridgeshire quite hard because of the rural nature of much of the county. A table was published showing petrol rationing limits:

- for cars up to 7 horse power 4 units or gallons per month
- for cars 8-9 horse power 5 units or gallons per month
- for cars up to 10-12 horse power 6 units or gallons per month
- for cars up to 13-15 horse power 7 units or gallons per month
- for cars up to 16-19 horse power 8 units or gallons per month
- for cars 20 horse power and upwards 10 units or gallons per month

The month didn't end well for many. On 27 September the first war tax was levied as well as an increase in income tax. The prices of food and petrol were also increasing in addition to extra taxes and the financial squeeze was beginning to hit hard.

The cancellation of Guy Fawkes celebrations in November had disappointed the children who had looked forward to building a bonfire, making the guy and watching him burn, then having a few fireworks, while potatoes were baked in the embers of the fire. Now Christmas was to be a muted affair. The authorities were keen to prevent what they termed frivolous spending when Britain needed every penny for the war effort. There was a campaign to encourage folk to put into war savings whatever they would have spent on Christmas presents. This was never going to achieve a 100 per cent success rate, but people did reduce their spending on gifts and Christmas decorations. Most toys during the war were either home-made or made from recycled materials. Even in peacetime there was not the expectation, as there is in the twenty-first century, of multiple and very expensive gifts to order. Many children were content with two or three small gifts, an orange and a few sweets.

External Christmas lights were banned due to the black-out and internal ones were discouraged because of the need to conserve energy materials. Christmas cards were not large or flamboyant, or even made of card. They were small, often home decorated, and on flimsy poor-quality paper. However, it was very much the thought that counted and those serving in the armed forces treasured their Christmas messages from loved ones without caring too much about the materials on which they were written. There were few luxury foodstuffs due to rationing, and the main festive dishes were either chicken or ham. In rural Cambridgeshire these might have been supplemented by rabbits or a brace of birds. However, not even Hitler could stop the carol concerts or the pantomimes celebrated in churches and schools. The BBC initiated a special Christmas Day programme on the radio in 1939, which, for the first time, included a special Christmas broadcast by King George VI. The Christmas broadcasts by the sovereign to his subjects proved so popular that they were continued after the war was over, and, when the king died in 1952, his daughter, Queen Elizabeth II, continued the tradition and has done so right up to the present day (2019).

Phoney War Ends,
Battle of Britain and the Blitz

Early in 1940 the Norway Campaign, a naval-based campaign by the Allies to seize neutral Norway, took place. It was foiled by the Germans in early April when they unexpectedly occupied Denmark and invaded Norway, forcing Allied troops to withdraw. Neville Chamberlain did not head a unified coalition government because neither Clement Attlee and the Labour Party nor David Lloyd George and the Liberals would support him. Attlee did not agree with him and Lloyd George was quite hostile, especially over the matter of his appeasement policies. The post-mortem debate on Norway began on 7 May and on 9 May Hitler invaded the Low Countries. The 'phoney war' was over and Chamberlain finally realised it was time for him to go. On 10 May he resigned as prime minister and advised the king to send for Winston Churchill who, as First Lord of the Admiralty, had been involved with naval battles during the period of the phoney war. By this time Chamberlain was not receiving a good press due to public perception that he was too trusting, perhaps too naïve, and had been 'played' by Hitler to Britain's detriment, in addition to the mishandling of the Norway campaign and other early wartime matters.

The whole business of powerful criticism and losing power depressed Chamberlain deeply, and his reputation was tarnished by what was now seen as his over eagerness to appease Germany instead of seeking other alliances and making more preparations for possible war. Neville Chamberlain died on 9 November 1940 almost six months to the day after his resignation from the premiership.

An airfield base was built on the northern edge of Waterbeach in 1940. It was a large base and came under the control of RAF Bomber Command for the duration of the war. Vickers Wellington and Short Stirling were initially the main types of plane which flew from this base; 1942 was the peak year for sorties by these aircraft from RAF Waterbeach, but by 1943 it had become a training base for No.514 Squadron of the RAF and they flew Avro Lancaster planes of the type which was used by the Dambusters on their famous German raids in May 1943.

Between 26 May and 4 June the legendary evacuation of Dunkerque (Dunkirk) took place. A British Expeditionary Force (BEF) had been sent to defend France but, after German forces invaded France, Belgium and Holland on 10 May, the BEF found itself trapped on the northern coast of France and withdrew to Dunkerque, the nearest reasonable port. The BEF was ultimately defeated, losing 68,000 soldiers to the French campaign along with most of its tanks and armoury. A kind of victory was snatched from the jaws of defeat by the rescue of 338,226 soldiers from the beaches of Normandy, using a flotilla of 800 boats of all shapes and sizes working alongside military craft. Churchill called their rescue *'a miracle of deliverance'* but warned against regarding Dunkerque as a victory.

Neither the city nor the county had much industry in which the Germans were interested but there were the railways and the airfields. A large railway network connected directly with London and ports on the East Coast. Munitions, military supplies to the large number of airfields in the county, industrial goods, food and medical provisions, coal, and a host of other items from the North and the Midlands, were transported from the huge marshalling yards at March (now part of Cambridgeshire but not during the war) via Cambridge to London. The south Cambridge/shire railways were often termed 'the backbone of the war effort', and it was this railway network which attracted unwelcome attention from the Germans.

The First Civilian Casualties

In June 1940 Cambridge experienced its first bombing raid but German intentions were generally better than the practical outcomes of German bombing campaigns. Consequently, the German planes managed to miss the railways altogether when they dropped a large number of high explosive bombs over Vicarage Terrace on the night of 18/19 June. Eleven people, including children, died, and there was a great deal of damage. These casualties were said to have been the first civilian casualties of the war on the British mainland and a defining end to the Phoney War. Loathe to give up their aim of attacking the railways in both the city and the county, the Germans attacked twice more in August. This time their bombs hit Fenners Cricket Ground, Leys Avenue, Pemberton Terrace and Shaftesbury Road, and they also hit fields in the county just outside the city. Once again, they missed their targets completely.

By now however the Battle of Britain was raging in which Cambridgeshire played an important part. Cambridgeshire is a fairly flat county, like neighbouring Suffolk and Norfolk, which acted as twin buffers between Cambridgeshire and

BOMBS NEXT DOOR — BUT SHE CARRIES ON!

Vicarage Terrace, Cambridge, bombing June 1940. (Courtesy of Cambridge Local Studies)

the East Coast. It was therefore an ideal choice for the RAF to site their airfields and installations. However, its more inland location was a reflection of its slightly lesser aerial importance. Norfolk had over forty Second World War airfields; Suffolk had thirty plus, while Cambridgeshire could only boast twenty-seven. Of course, it was a smaller county, but the main threat was always going to be to the coast, and the airfields proved to be the other chief target of German bombers.

Cambridge had Marshall Airport in Teversham on the outskirts of Cambridge, which opened in 1937 and expanded during the war towards Newmarket Road. A car and vehicle business was established there in 1909 by David G. Marshall and the firm made its debut in aviation when in 1912 their mechanics helped repair the engine of a British Army airship which had made an emergency landing. Marshall's was a large engineering works and the airport became a key centre for training air crews. Over 20,000 of these trainees fought in the war including Johnnie Johnson, the top scoring British fighter ace. To the disgust of many

Spitfire, Marshall's airfield, 1944.

male pilots, Marshall's had a number of female pilots who delivered planes from factories or flew them between inland airbases, often flying solo.. They were not allowed to fly into combat, but they flew cargo planes between various airports and delivered new war planes to their destinations.

One of the better known was Freydis Sharland who often flew into Marshall's Airport. Born in Cambridge, she had initially trained as a Red Cross nurse in Colchester at the outbreak of war, but in 1942 she joined the Air Transport Auxiliary (ATA). She did her training on Magisters and twin-engined Ansons, after which she flew Spitfires and Hurricanes, as well as Vickers Wellington, Lockheed Hudson and de Havilland Mosquito planes. Her favourite was always the Spitfire because it was *'light, neat and compact'*. She learned to navigate in bad weather and to avoid barrage balloons without navigational aids or radio equipment. All she had was a map and she was told to always fly below cloud. However, this was not necessarily easy or wise if flying over hilly territory. Despite her flying skills she was sometimes denied access to the officers' mess just because she was female, and one man simply refused to fly with her because he said he was not going to be flown by a woman. The inequality and sexism annoyed her greatly, but she tried to ignore it because of her love of flying.

The Battle of Britain

The county of Cambridgeshire had a number of sizeable RAF bases, including those at Bassingbourn, Bottisham, Bourn, Castle Camps, Duxford, Fowlmere,

Little Staughton, Mepal, Oakington, Snailwell, Steeple Morden, Upwood, Warboys, Waterbeach and Wratting Common. RAF Bassingbourn had opened in 1938 before the declaration of war and is still in use as a military site, well camouflaged by woods and natural vegetation. In April 1940 a single German raider attacked the airfield and dropped ten bombs causing damage to direction-finding and wireless-transmitter equipment. This was followed in August by a further attack in which a single bomb hit the barracks block, killing eleven men and injuring a further fifteen. RAF Duxford had been established since the end of the First World War and became one of the largest airfield bases in Cambridgeshire, but a telling statistic is that the average life expectancy of an RAF pilot flying from RAF Duxford was just eleven days. Around fifty to sixty Spitfires and Hurricanes flew every day from RAF Duxford and from RAF Fowlmere which was established in 1940 as a fighter squadron airfield. They were both operational in the Battle of Britain.

RAF bases at Bottisham, Castle Camps and Oakington were also established in 1940. RAF Bottisham eventually became a USAAF fighter airfield. RAF Castle Camps was also a fighter airfield which lay near the Cambridgeshire-Suffolk border. The first incendiary bombs to be dropped by the Luftwaffe on Cambridgeshire landed near Duxford in early June, shortly before the attack on Vicarage Terrace in the city of Cambridge. Then, in mid-August another 220 bombs, a record total, hit the Duxford area. RAF Upwood was also hit several times by Luftwaffe bombs but sustained only minor damage. In September there was great excitement when

Bassingbourn barracks, opened March 1938

a Ju88 bomber crash landed at RAF Oakington after being attacked by Hurricane fighters. RAF Oakington was home to No.7 Squadron from 1940-1945 but it was also used for No.218 Squadron during 1940. Like at Bottisham, the grass surfaces at RAF Oakington caused take-off and landing problems for the heavier planes such as Stirlings. Finally, in 1941 and 1942, proper runways were built and RAF Oakington was able to expand and cope with heavier traffic.

RAF Little Staughton was a small airfield built in 1941 which was used by the RAF and, from 1942-1944, by the USAAF, but it was of less significance than many of the Cambridgeshire airfields. RAF Snailwell, close to the Suffolk border, was a sizeable airfield and a number of RAF Squadrons operated from there including Nos. 56, 137, 152, 160, 178, 181, 182, 183, 184, 247, 268, 309, 527, 613. It was also home to the RAF Belgian training school and the USAAF 41st Base Complement Squadron, 51st Service Squadron; the 9th Fighter Command Unit, which carried out massive air attacks on D-Day with P-51 Mustang and P-47 Thunderbolt fighters and the USAAF 350th and 347th Fighter Groups. In addition, RAF Snailwell had the distinction of holding No.1426 (Enemy Aircraft) Flight to evaluate aircraft captured from the Luftwaffe.

The Battle of Britain raged from 10 July to 31 October 1940. It was the first major victory of the Allies and marked a turning point in the war. *'Never in the field of human conflict was so much owed by so many to so few,'* declared Churchill and he was right. Hitler and the Luftwaffe had expected to win this battle and to force England into submission. Their failure to do so was incredibly demoralising for the German High Command. Much of the Battle of Britain was fought in the skies over southern England

Pilot with Cambridge Spitfire, Nov 1942. (Courtesy of Cambridge Local Studies)

but hundreds of planes from airfields in Cambridgeshire and

other East Anglian RAF bases provided invaluable back-up and support, as well as policing the English Channel and the North Sea. Training was tough. Pilots not only had to master aircraft controls and flying techniques, they had to learn to fly in all sorts of conditions and over all sorts of terrain. The landscape and skies over southern England presented relatively few problems and it became a regular practice to send air crews or lone pilots on circular missions which involved take-off from base, flying up country to the west, turn around at a northern destination, flying back to base down country to the east. Many of these circular training flight routes involved time over hills, notably the southern Pennines and the Peak District. If pilots were going to fly across France and attack Germany, they needed experience of flying in all weathers and over high ground.

The technology of the wartime planes was much simpler and more limited than those of today. A major problem was that cockpits weren't pressurised, and altimeters could be seriously affected by air pressure to the extent that readings given could be incorrect by 100ft (over 30m) or more. Night flying in winter was difficult; fog, rain and snow often obscured the hills, both at night and in the daytime, causing disorientation, and the Peak District, particularly the Dark Peak, which is noted for its sudden changes of weather, became infamous as a 'graveyard of planes'. A young pilot from Duxford, on a training flight to Kirkbride, became lost over the Derbyshire hills. His fuel was running low and he abandoned the plane. Although he was unhurt, the plane crashed near Edale, in the highest part of the Peak District, and was badly damaged. The crew of another aircraft, which took off from RAF Warboys bound for Warrington in Cheshire, tried to fly beneath the cloud cover and flew straight into the ground, again near Edale. The plane was wrecked but, amazingly, none of the four crew were seriously hurt.

Training flight crashes in Cambridgeshire, however, were mercifully, comparatively rare until the Americans arrived, but there were tragedies which occurred. The best known occurred in what is now the north of the county at Holme Lode Great Fen, near Huntingdon, although in the Second World War this was not a part of Cambridgeshire, as Huntingdonshire was then a separate county. A Spitfire, flown by a young Brighton pilot, Harold Penketh, crashed into the fen in 1940. Harold Penketh was just 20 and had only thirteen hours flying experience. The reason for the crash is not definitively known, but he had broken away from his squadron and it is thought that his oxygen supply may have failed, causing him to become unconscious and slump over the controls. The crash site is in remote countryside, on the edge of dense woodland, and it is believed the plane simply flew into the ground after its pilot lost consciousness. There is a small on-site memorial to him acknowledging his sacrifice to the war.

Italians Interned and PoW Camps

On 10 June Italy, under the leadership of Benito Mussolini, joined the war on the side of Germany. There were a number of Italian communities in England. The Italians were sociable people who had integrated well with their English neighbours, some had married English girls and taken on British citizenship, and some had served in the First World War with the British forces, so it came as a great shock to discover that suddenly they were the enemy. Where before there had been only welcome and friendliness there were now riots against the 'Italian enemies'. Churchill saw them as a national security threat and ordered the internment of every Italian male aged between 17 and 60. The men were arrested and taken away, leaving their wives and children in tears without any form of support. Some of them even had sons serving in the British Army. Despite their protestations of loyalty all Italian men were questioned about their loyalties and whether they supported the *Fascisti*. The answers given appear to have been irrelevant because they were all interned.

There were not many prisoner of war (PoW) camps in Cambridgeshire. It was practice to site the camps in remote areas away from centres of population where transport and communications would be limited, thereby rendering escape much more difficult. Cambridgeshire had its remote areas, but it also had a number of vulnerable airfields and it was too close for comfort to the airfields of Norfolk and Suffolk and to the East Coast which offered a means of escape by boat that would be difficult to detect. Having said that, in the wartime county of Cambridgeshire, there are only three recorded PoW camps and all three were close to built-up areas of population. One was on Hauxton Road in Trumpington, on the edge of Cambridge; the other two were in Ely. Trumpington PoW camp, camp No.45, held both Italian and German prisoners, although initially the prisoners would have been mainly Italian. They were not seen as such a threat because many of them had already been accepted into English society and had been viewed as friends until Mussolini's intervention. Many of the Italians worked on nearby farms and, after the war was over, lodged with local farmers.

After 1943 the camp held German prisoners, but by the end of the war, its prisoners were exclusively Austrian. The site is close to the present day (2019) Trumpington Meadows housing project. Barton Field Camp in Ely, camp No.26, held German PoWs. This site is now lost under new housing and a golf course. After Churchill had ordered the internment of all Italian men over the age of 16, secure accommodation had to be provided for them quickly. West Fen Militia Camp, near West Fen Road in Ely, camp No.130, now covered by Priors Court, held Italian PoWs, guarded by civilians rather than soldiers.

Friday Bridge Agricultural Camp

Site of former prison camp in north Cambridgeshire during the war.

British summer time (BST), the daylight hours saving scheme adopted in 1916, had continued, but at the end of 1940 the clocks were not put back an hour to Greenwich Mean Time (GMT), as was the custom, but remained on BST. In the spring of 1941, the clocks were put forward by another hour so that the country was then two hours ahead of GMT. This was dubbed British Double Summer Time (BDST) which remained in force until autumn 1945. In the winter clocks were put back an hour to BST but did not return to GMT until after the war.

The mood was generally sombre and there was little heart for Christmas cheer. The children looked forward to it as the one festive occasion they were still permitted to enjoy, although for the evacuees and refugees there was sadness at being parted from their parents and families at Christmastime. Christmas spending nose-dived, although £10 million (just under £500,000,000) of war bonds were bought nationwide in the week before Christmas which, together with the proceeds of the 'war week' held in Cambridge earlier in the year, added a substantial contribution to national war funds. Most presents were home-made and many were simply for the children. Small dolls houses, toy soldiers, or model ships made from bits of wood, or knitted dolls and teddy bears, were favourites. The most popular present for adults was a bar of soap. Scant rations of ham, bacon, suet, butter and margarine were saved for the main meal and home-grown vegetables (in season British vegetables would include mainly potatoes, parsnips, onions, cabbage, kale and sprouts) and home-made pickles or chutneys would accompany Christmas dinner. Puddings were made without fruit, nuts or marzipan. Alcohol and nuts were prohibitively expensive.

Cheese was strictly rationed. Apples and pears were the only British fruits in season and these were scarce. There were, however, extra rations of tea and sugar in the week before Christmas; but in rural Cambridgeshire, there was always something to be had from the countryside, such as rabbits, pigeons, herbs and wild raspberries. However, any form of travel was discouraged; partly due to petrol rationing; partly due to the need to keep the roads and railways available for the transportation of troops and war supplies.

The BBC did their best to add a little gaiety to proceedings, broadcasting variety shows, the King's Speech, a programme called 'Kitchen Front' (broadcast daily at 8am involving issues of rationing, use of available foods, trying new wartime recipes, discouraging food waste etc) and a sermon from the cathedral ruins in Coventry. Christmas church services continued as normal, but bells could not be rung (as this would signify invasion) and windows could not be lit up. Cinema celebrated Christmas with the release of *The Great Dictator* starring Charlie Chaplin, a film which poked satirical fun at Hitler. In one scene, Chaplin, dressed as Hitler, his hair and moustache an absolute brilliantined copy, shinned up a floor-to-ceiling curtain, clutching a small globe, announcing to his startled lieutenants below '*I want to be alone!*' Hitler was beyond furious when he learned of the film and it is rumoured that Charlie Chaplin was at the top of his blacklist for when, as Hitler believed, he would conquer England.

Rationing, Restrictions, Resources and the RAF

RAF Duxford was becoming a large and important airfield. One of the most crucial decisions of the war was made here when a British test pilot, Ronald Harker, succeeded in convincing Air Ministry officials to replace the Allison engines used in the P51-Mustangs with the superior Rolls-Royce Merlin engines. These gave the aircraft greater power and manoeuvrability and enabled them to fly up to 42,00ft (12,802m), instead of the previous 15,000ft (4,572m) limitation, making them excellent fighter escorts.

The construction of airfields continued into 1941 as the air raids intensified. RAF Bourn was opened in 1941, as a bomber airfield, the same year as RAF Waterbeach, and this airfield, like RAF Oakington, would remain in use and operational for over seventy years, although in later years RAF Waterbeach came under the control of the Army. RAF Mepal, however, was one of the more unusual wartime airfields in that it did not officially open until 1943 and then it was used exclusively by the 75th (New Zealand) Squadron.

There was also a large RAF hospital built at Ely which specialised in treating burn injuries because those whose planes crashed often suffered terrible injuries. One of the worst burn tragedies occurred at West Wickham in July 1943. A Stirling BF504 had just taken off, but then side-slipped, probably due to wind strength, crashed and exploded. Two airmen, who were sitting outside having a brew after their lunch, saw it happen and dashed across to the burning wreckage. The seven members of the air crew had escaped the plane, but they were all on fire, screaming with pain and rolling on the ground desperately trying to put out the flames. The two airmen rushed from one to the other helping to put out the flames and burning their hands and lower arms in the process. Ambulances rushed over to help the injured but two of the crew died before they could reach them. The remaining five and the two wounded airmen who had helped them were loaded into the ambulances which headed rapidly for the Ely RAF hospital. On the way they were stopped at a level crossing but one of the ambulance crew got out and explained what had happened to the signalman who then held up the train to let the ambulance through. Sadly, his efforts were in vain. Three more of

The RAF Hospital at Ely now known as The Princess of Wales Hospital.

the crew had died by the time the ambulance reached the hospital. The remaining two crew members were dead on arrival in the treatment rooms. The two airmen were treated for burns to their hands and returned to West Wickham in a state of shock and grief.

Today the RAF hospital is known as the Princess of Wales Hospital and it has lots of smart new buildings, but a part of the former RAF wartime hospital can still be detected at its centre. Plane crashes were all too frequent as the fighting continued, and there were plenty of badly injured pilots who needed complex treatments although not all of them were the result of enemy action. A Tiger Moth on a training flight spiralled down into woodlands near Hardwick and exploded. One of the crew members escaped with minor injuries and shock, but the pilot was killed, charred beyond recognition. A Mosquito, coming into land at Bourn airfield, crashed and burst into flames, killing the pilot instantly, and a Wellington bomber crashed as it was coming into land at RAF Bassingbourn, killing two of the crew. Soon afterwards a Short Stirling aircraft preparing to land at RAF Oakington caught fire and crashed at Dry Drayton. RAF Bourn and RAF Oakington were strafed repeatedly by the Luftwaffe which caused a lot of damage but, fortunately, little loss of life.

August, however, was a more tragic month, when the Luftwaffe shot down three bombers over Cambridgeshire airbases. The first, on 12 August, involved a Blenheim bomber which had taken off from RAF Upwood on a night training exercise. It was shot down and crashed near Wilburton, killing all the crew. A week later a Wellington bomber was shot down near Barrington, and the following day, yet another Wellington bomber fell victim to German fighter planes as it came into land at RAF Bassingbourn.

By the time the Americans entered the war, after Pearl Harbor was bombed by the Japanese in December 1941, Lancaster and Hampden bombers were already a fairly common sight but, after the arrival of the Americans, the skies suddenly seemed to become '*positively crowded*', according to one Cambridgeshire schoolboy, '*with Fortresses, Liberators, Bostons, Dakotas, Mustangs, Lightnings and Thunderbolts*', but at least they were '*friendly planes*'. East Anglia was ideal for siting American airbases with its huge number of flat acres and its proximity to the European coast. Several Cambridgeshire airfields were shared, notably Duxford (airbase for a number of Super Fortresses) and Bassingbourn, by both the RAF and the USAAF, and RAF Bottisham which was finally taken over by the USAAF in 1943.

Flying Fortress, Duxford airfield.

The Blitz and Air Raid Shelters

The London Blitz lasted from 7 September 1940 until 11 May 1941. From 7 September the capital was bombed for fifty-seven consecutive days and nights. The attacks caused widespread loss of life with over 40,000 dead and another 46,000 injured, enormous damage and lowering of general morale. Hitler's policy of *Blitzkreig*, German for 'lightning war', was based on speed, surprise, co-ordination and rapid mass attacks on an area to cause maximum destruction, damage to infrastructure, chaos and panic. Consequently, in order to try and protect London from further attacks, a decision was taken to build decoy sites, known as 'Starfish sites', in remote parts of the countryside. RAF Balloon Command were in charge of the Starfish sites. The project was an extension of a decoy programme designed to protect airfields and factories devised by Colonel John Turner, and decoy targets were intended to confuse German bombers into thinking they were bombing a city when, in fact, they were bombing empty countryside.

Each 'Starfish site' (or Special Fire site from which they took their name) had an air raid shelter for the operational crew and several different devices to simulate lights and fire. The sites were usually built between 4 miles (7km) and 10 miles (17km) from the place they were intended to protect and at least a mile (1.75km) from any village or settlement. Vehicle tracks could be faked by spraying pesticide onto surrounding grass and heather. Glow boxes simulated city lights. 'Fire baskets' on stands about 20ft (6m) tall contained fires of creosote or coal onto which petrol or diesel was dripped from overhead tanks to simulate exploding incendiary bombs hitting buildings after the attacking planes had passed over. Up to 30 tons of fuel could be stored on site for this purpose. Water was then pumped onto the fires giving clouds of steam which looked like smoke. The 'lights' and 'fires' were controlled from concrete bunkers. Cambridge, painfully aware of its proximity to London, decided that the city should also have Starfish protection even though it had not suffered any Blitz damage. Some of the protective Starfish sites were to be built in the Cambridgeshire countryside, but not in the numbers designed to protect cities like London, Manchester, Sheffield and Liverpool because Cambridge, although Marshall's was involved in aircraft production and the Pye Group were involved in war work, was not perceived by the Germans to have the same amount of heavy industry or strategic importance as the larger cities. The main targets within Cambridgeshire and the city of Cambridge, since Hitler had forbidden the bombing of the university, were the lines of communication (primarily the railways) and the airfields.

Cambridgeshire is pretty flat countryside, especially near the fenlands, so that even a railway bridge stands out and can be fairly easily spotted. German practice was often to follow railway lines in towards their targets. Although the blackout was strictly enforced, on clear moonlit nights, or even on bright starlit nights, rails might be clearly visible, glinting in the darkness, and light was reflected on water, rivers, dykes, and 'tank traps' (deep water-filled ditches), of which there were a number in Cambridgeshire. In mid-January, over 200 incendiary bombs were dropped on Hills Road and Regent Street, about half a mile (0.8km) from the railway station, setting the Perse School on fire. This was followed up two weeks later by an attack on the area around the Mill Road railway bridge, which is probably where the Germans had been aiming in the earlier attack. Two railway cottages were hit, killing two people and injuring another eleven. A month later, Cherry Hinton Road and Hills Road, from the Catholic Church to Station Road, were heavily bombed but the bombs missed the station and the marshalling yards. In early May there was another attempt to bomb the railway, but again they were way off target, bombing the area between Hills Road and Trumpington Road. Although they hit fifty houses, only five caught fire and there were no fatalities. Yet another attempt was made on the Mill Road bridge area on 29 August when ten high explosive bombs fell on Great Eastern Street. This resulted in another two deaths and seven people injured, but the railways remained undamaged. Clearly dispirited, the Germans then gave up attacking the city and the county for almost a year.

It had been quickly realised that air-raid shelters built at ground level did not offer much protection and that it was safer to be underground. In the Spanish Civil War, Barcelona, which had become a Republican (freedom fighters) stronghold, suffered heavy bombing from the Germans and the Italians. The Spanish have a very creative streak and it was in Barcelona that the first underground bomb-proof shelters were built. These initial shelters were built as a network of tunnels cut into the native bedrock. They were fitted with benches, toilets, electric lighting run from batteries, and first aid equipment. Several British engineers visited Barcelona to study the effects of bombing and the construction of the underground shelters. One scientist, J.B.S. Haldane, wrote:

There were four entrances which led down by ramps with a few steps to the tunnels. The ramps twisted repeatedly, until a depth of about 55 feet below the ground was reached. Here began a labyrinth of passages about 7 feet high by 4 feet broad. They were cut in the very tough soil of the district, and had no lining, and I think no supports such as pit props. They were, however, being lined with tiles with a cement backing so at to give a semi-circular arch and vertical walls.

The idea of using tunnels as air raid shelters, like those of the Underground in London, caught on quickly after the commencement of hostilities, and the image of a warm, well-lit, safe place with companionable chatter over cups of tea, a space to sleep and toilet facilities persisted long after the war was over. Cambridgeshire did not have tunnel systems, although churches often had crypts and civic buildings usually had cellars, but, generally, more simple and economic underground shelters had to be used. One of the most popular shelters was the Anderson shelter, named after its designer, Sir John Anderson. These measured 6ft 6ins (1.95m) by 4ft 6ins (1.35m) and were made from six curved and corrugated iron sheets bolted together which were then half buried in the earth of people's gardens. The entrance would be protected by 'a steel shield and an earthen blast wall'. However, these shelters were often damp, cramped and cold. Lack of sleep and boredom were major factors. There was also the Stanton Shelter, named after the manufacturers, which were segments of reinforced concrete, interlocked and bolted together then partially buried; but these were used mainly on airfields. In any case, Cambridgeshire was a mainly rural county and communal shelters were not always practical, although there was a bunker-type of air raid shelter at Duxford close to the airfield, and a 'blast pen'. Blast pens were designed to protect aircraft and personnel away from the main airfield buildings, although they were mostly built on Fighter Command airfields. The E-shaped pens were constructed from concrete which was protected by banked earth. Each of the two bays gave parked aircraft some shelter from flying debris in an air raid. The bays were roofless, but the 'long spine' of the E usually enclosed a narrow air raid shelter for air crews and maintenance staff. Most of the larger airfields, like RAF Bassingbourn, RAF Fowlmere and RAF Waterbeach, usually had some sort of shelter for protection of their own staff.

Public civilian air raid shelters were there for whoever needed them. Ely had larger communal air raid shelters for its schools and evacuees. Whittlesford had an air raid shelter near the railway station. A more unlikely setting for an air raid shelter was in the grounds of the Tudor period Sawston Hall where Mary, Queen of Scots, was said to have sheltered. Remote farms and scattered hamlets scarcely bothered, preferring to shelter under the stairs or a table, although in the larger villages some people had an Anderson shelter which they would share with neighbours. The alternative was the Morrison shelter, designed by John Baker and named after the Home Secretary of the day, Herbert Morrison. This was rather like a big steel dog cage measuring 6ft (2m) long by 4ft (1.2m) wide by 2ft 6ins (.75m) high. It was placed in a downstairs room, often the kitchen, where the top could be used as a table. A mattress was usually put inside for comfort and people sheltered there during raids since it could supposedly withstand tons of falling rubble, but they could prove very claustrophobic.

Within the city of Cambridge there were a number of communal air raid shelters. There was one built specially for the residents of Gwydir Street because the houses were too small to readily accommodate Morrison shelters and the gardens were too small for Anderson shelters. On Coleridge Road there is a bunker covered in graffiti and almost completely hidden by foliage, a former air raid shelter which offered some shelter from bombing to people in that area, but the entrance is now blocked up. The St Regis flats, newly built in 1939 on Chesterton Road, advertised, as a selling point, that there were built-in air raid shelters. However, the building was requisitioned as the base of the East Anglian Regional Commissioner for Civil Defence, Sir William Spens, who was Master of Corpus Christi College. Today (2019) it is owned by Clare College and used as student accommodation.

Air raid shelters were built for use by Marshall's airfield on Newmarket Road and public air raid shelters were built on Christ's Pieces, Parker's Piece in front of Regent Terrace, and along the banks of the river Cam at Jesus Green near the bridge. There was also an air raid shelter in the orchard of Jesus College. A shelter was built beneath the central Market Square and old wine cellars, built in the eighteenth century below a hostelry on the adjoining Peas Hill and capable of holding around 250 people, were used as well. Trenches were dug into Midsummer Common and lined with concrete. In addition, brick shelters were built for the children of Park Street School near the brook on Jesus Green. There is usually little trace left of Second World War air raid shelters, but during the long hot dry summer of 2018 grass parch marks appeared, showing the siting, size and shape of the subterranean air raid shelters on Jesus Green.

It was necessary to have rules and regulations for the larger public shelters, but these were mostly simple common sense. Smoking was prohibited. Animals could not be brought in although this caused some considerable distress to those who still owned treasured cats or dogs. Lighting was not to be altered or other equipment touched. Any unnecessary movement was to be avoided which was hard on the children. No litter was to be left. The instructions of the shelter warden were to be obeyed at all times and when the 'All Clear' signal was given, people were to leave in an orderly manner.

Women at Work

Although women were once again doing many of the men's jobs, they still suffered discrimination and they did not get the same pay for the same work and this lack of equality led to further protest. A minimum wage £3 (£135) for men was expected but for women it was only £2 (£90). Three days paid holiday for everyone were also included. The women of Cambridgeshire were reacting to this new war in pretty much the same way as they had reacted to the First World War. They knew it was their job to keep the home fires burning, as the popular slogan went, to cook good meals from scant ingredients, to work in their gardens or on allotments, 'digging for victory' as Churchill had asked them to do, and growing as much food as they could, caring for their children, and helping in some way with the war effort. There was (and still is) a belief that the only real work is paid work. This ignores the fact that much, if not most, of the work done in Britain during the Second World War was unpaid and done mainly by women. Women fulfilled roles of housewives, mothers, volunteers, helpers etc. They were responsible for cooking, cleaning, washing, making or mending clothes for their families, bringing up the children, volunteering to help with the war effort, helping in air raids or with evacuations, providing treats for the troops…the list was endless and all the jobs were unpaid.

If a woman had children under 14 (the school leaving age) at home she was not required to work outside the home at a paid 'day job'. However, the contributions made by these women were not only valuable but essential to the smooth running and mobilisation of the country and its fighting force. Even if they did paid or voluntary work, their domestic responsibilities remained central to their lives. However, from 1941 female conscription meant that women were also conscripted into work in factories. Despite conscription, large numbers of men were free with their complaints if their wives were out working and dinner not on the table when they returned home. The home was not as they would like it. Sometimes their children were being fed from tins and not being looked after or disciplined properly as they saw it. Even worse, some women could earn more than their husbands, and, in the men's eyes, this was shameful indeed.

Britain was the most completely mobilised country in the Second World War. Although women now had full electoral representation and a much wider choice of work and lifestyle than in the First World War, they were still seen as somehow inferior beings by many men and incapable of the same intelligence and initiative, despite the numbers of them working in skilled or dangerous jobs and at the top-secret decoding centre in Bletchley Park.

British Restaurants and Rationing

Food rationing was strict, although potatoes and vegetables were not rationed and nor was bread, at least not until after the war. Fruit supplies were extremely limited. However, Churchill, following Lloyd George's example in the First World War, had ordered the establishment of communal kitchens, or 'British Restaurants' as he preferred to call them, almost from the moment war was declared. The main advantages of these kitchens were that they could bulk buy fresh food more economically; use far less fuel by cooking numbers of meals on one cooker, thereby eliminating the need for individual meals to be cooked on individual cookers in individual homes; and provide cheap hot meals for military personnel, office and factory employees, students, evacuees and hard-pressed working mothers. There was usually a choice of five meat dishes, five vegetables and five desserts. Popular savoury dishes included hotpots, roast meats, stews, pies and potatoes in any shape or form; preferred desserts were often rice pudding, jam roly-poly or spotted dick (usually a suet-based pudding with dried fruit). Bread and prune pudding or sultana and carrot pudding were also wartime dessert options which would not be to modern tastes. A standard meal of meat and two vegetables followed by a pudding would cost 9d (around £1.70). Catering allowances per individual, per main meal were a little Spartan by twenty-first century standards. An ounce equals just over 28g. The average allocations per person for caterers providing main meals of the day for people were:

0.14 oz of bacon
0.30 oz of fats
0.12 oz sugar
1 oz meat
0.32 oz fish
0.21 oz cheese
0.14 oz preserves
0.16 oz dried eggs
0.12 oz skimmed milk powder
0.67 oz sausage meat
The total weight of food allowance is 3.18 oz (just over 90g).

By contemporary comparison a McDonald's quarter pounder, often seen as a snack in 2018, includes 4oz (113.4g) of meat plus salad or cheese and various dressings. British Restaurants served their meals in decently furnished cafes which carried no hint of charity. As Lloyd George had discovered, proper nutrition was essential for a healthy and efficient workforce. Also, as in the First World War, those doing heavy industrial work were allowed higher meat and sugar rations. The restaurants, usually staffed by members of the WVS, were open to all members of the public, but Churchill was heavily criticised by the right wing of his own party who declared that *'communal feeding was entirely abhorrent to the British way of life'* and protested throughout the war and beyond about the matter. Churchill turned a deaf ear. Boarding schools, colleges, factories, larger retail stores, offices, schools, military establishments, country house staff and servants, often had their own canteens or dining rooms and most people enjoyed some company and conversation while they ate their meals.

Eighty years later, communal eating has not disappeared and it is being actively encouraged by some restaurants. This is because eating is also a social activity, and it has been ever since pre-historic hunters dragged their kill back home to roast over a communal fire, after which it was shared among their tribe or family and eaten with fruit or berries picked by their womenfolk. A Dorset bakery, in one of the coastal towns popular with visitors, divided their huge kitchen area in half. In one half they baked a variety of breads, rolls, pastries and cakes each morning. In the other half communal tables and wooden benches were set out. Freshly baked goods were laid out on the counter for breakfast along with butter, preserves, honey, cheese, fruit and yoghurt. Self-service toasters, kettles and coffee machines were also provided. Customers, from all walks of life, paid £5 each and ate their fill, making new friends around the tables as they did so. It became so popular that, eventually, only early birds managed to get a seat, but it amply illustrates that communal feeding is not *'entirely abhorrent to the British way of life'*, and may actually be enjoyable to a sizeable section of the populace.

The food minister, Lord Woolton, was certainly in favour of the British restaurants, and pointed out that an additional factor for their establishment and use was the disruption of gas, water and electricity supplies as a result of the bombing raids. Although the city of Cambridge had four or five 'communal kitchens' in the First World War, and a couple of British restaurants in the Second World War, the social ethos in the city seemed to have changed by the 1940s and, despite rationing, there was not quite the same enthusiasm. In the county of Cambridgeshire, British restaurants were virtually a non-starter anyway because low population density and the lack of transport meant that there was little demand or necessity. Nevertheless, by 1943 there were over 2,000 British restaurants across the country serving up around 600,000 meals each day, each costing 9d (£1.70). However, in several cases, works canteens had taken the place of communal restaurants in many of the larger industrial cities and, although this increased the burden for women yet again, there was also an increasingly marked preference for home cooking rather than mass produced meals. A lesser complaint was that potatoes were always served as part of the British Restaurant meals and a sizeable number of people insisted that they often preferred bread with their meals instead.

Make Do and Mend 1944. (Courtesy of Cambridge Local Studies)

Make Do and Mend

On 1 June the Limitation of Supplies (Cloth and Apparel) Order was passed and civilian clothing was rationed for the first time. This was an effort both to conserve raw materials and free up workers and manufacturers for the production of items necessary for the war, especially munitions. Purchases of all types of clothing for everyone were subject to ration coupons in the same way as food. It was hard to keep up with fashions or growing children. The Board of Trade sponsored several ranges of 'utility clothing' which had strict specifications on the amounts of material to be used and the labour involved. No turn-ups were allowed on trousers, nor were double breasted suits permitted. Skirt and coat lengths were regulated. All utility clothing carried a label stating 'CC41'. This stood for Controlled Commodity and 41 referred to the year this measure had been instigated. Leading fashion designers, like Norman Hartnell and Hardy Amies, were commissioned to design clothing for the utility ranges and maximum prices chargeable for both cloth and clothing were laid down. Women became adept at 'make do and mend' by using old clothes and curtains to make new items of wear or by adorning faded clothes with bits of lace or ribbon.

Some items, such as silk or nylon stockings, were difficult, if not impossible, to obtain. Many girls and women either wore ankle socks or nothing with their shoes. The armed forces and school uniforms relied on thick lisle stockings which were simply for regulation purposes, and, in winter, warmth, but they were not popular. Most nylon stockings still had vertical seams along their backs and those wanting to dress up and look chic emulated these stocking seams by drawing them down their legs with eyeliner pencils or charcoal. Lines of 'national footwear' were also produced although the height of heels was strictly limited. Women became very adept at making clothes for themselves and their families. In addition, there was a clothing points system, which in 1941, was sixty-six points per annum. This system was governed by the amount of materials and labour involved in an individual item of clothing. Points had to be paid as well as cash for each item of clothing and clothing could not be bought without sufficient points allocation. A dress might cost eleven points while a man's suit cost twenty-four points, and a woollen coat cost eighteen points. In 1942 the number of points would be cut to forty-eight points annually; further reduced to thirty-six points in 1943 and by 1945 the annual allocation of clothing points was down to just twenty-four points per person.

Rationing and utility regulations might govern commercial supplies of clothing, but no-one could tell a housewife what to do with a pair of her old curtains or a dress that she would never wear again. 'Hand-me downs' became a well-used, if disliked, phrase. Clothes made or obtained for a first child would be handed down to siblings. Hems would be taken up and down. Waistbands would be taken in…or out. Trousers would be lengthened or shortened. Coat and dress seams would be altered. The system of hand-me downs seemed to be particularly hard for teenage girls and young women who simply longed for something new of their own to wear. There were propaganda campaigns encouraging people to follow the rules on rationing, to economise on travel and to walk whenever it was possible instead of using transport, to salvage whatever they could and to save all waste paper. Sons and daughters would scoff as they watched their mother or father saving every little thing, like bits of string, pieces of paper, elastic bands, scraps of material etc. that they thought might come in useful one day, but they often found themselves grateful for their parents' forethought and thrift.

Thrift and economy were also key words for wartime weddings. One of the major reasons for people choosing to marry in wartime was because the groom was due to be sent to fight overseas. White weddings were often considered inappropriate because of the material resources needed for the bride's dress and those of the bridesmaids. Old or spare parachute silk was keenly sought, but a bride was considered fortunate indeed if she managed to obtain any. The women of Cambridgeshire counted themselves especially fortunate because so many airfields were based in their county that they stood some chance of obtaining at least a little parachute silk. However, wedding outfits were most likely to be day dresses or two-piece suits which could also be worn on many other occasions. Church bells could not be rung to celebrate weddings because bell ringing was reserved for the threat of invasion or dire emergency. Film was scarce and brides were lucky if they got even a couple of photographs of their wedding. Ration coupons were pooled so that a modest wedding cake could be made and the wedding breakfast, if there was one, was usually limited to immediate family of no more than about a dozen people and was often a simple meal of sausages and mash or a savoury pie. Traditionally there would just be a small slice of cake and a cup of tea for those who had attended the wedding. Many couples had no proper honeymoon but the more fortunate might manage a couple of nights in a hotel. If a bride was rostered to do fire-watching duties it could be very difficult to change shifts and a number of brides spent their wedding night scanning the skies, watching for planes and falling bombs. Fire-watching duties could be lonely, cold, tiring, frightening, but never romantic.

Radio, cinema and dances were the main forms of entertainment although transport to events could be difficult for those who lived in the more outlying parts of the county. However, many of the Cambridgeshire villages had a village hall within walking distance where dances could be held, and in some a makeshift screen would be erected to show films. Margaret Mitchell's classic story of the American Civil War, *Gone with the Wind*, made in 1939, starring Clark Gable and Vivian Leigh, was the most popular film of the Second World War. Radio, however, was generally the chief form of entertainment and news. The BBC had just two programmes: the Home Service (today's equivalent is Radio 4) and the Forces Programme. The BBC news was one of the main means of communication of events. Much of it was war news of air raids, land and sea battles, plus the general progress of the war, although there was some home front news as well. Singer Vera Lynn, known as the Forces' Sweetheart, was one of the most popular entertainers. By 1945 there were 10,000,000 radio licences held in Britain. Wartime radios were quite cumbersome in comparison to modern sets. They worked by valves and were enclosed in polished wooden cases, the speaker covered in a kind of hessian. There were usually just two knobs on the front: one for volume and on/off facilities; the other was used to search for radio stations.

On 7 December the Japanese bombed Pearl Harbor which was, from their point of view, a victory, but it cost the Germans dearly because America entered the war and Britain no longer stood alone. A week before Christmas the British Government passed the National Service (No.2) Act. All men and women aged 18-60 were now liable for national service, which included military service for those under the age of 51. It was the first time women had been conscripted and it was also the first military registration of those aged 18½.

It also raised the question of conscientious objectors once more. The legislation had made provision for people to object to fighting on moral grounds. There were nearly four times as many conscientious objectors as during the First World War and there was a register of conscientious objectors containing around 6,000 names of which about a third were women. They came from all walks of life and all strata of society. The whole question of conscientious objectors was a difficult one. During the Second World War there were three main grounds: religious, moral and political. Most objectors fell into the first two categories, although a few of the Cambridge intelligentsia tried to put up cleverly complicated arguments. There was a three-tier system: they could be registered unconditionally, registered as willing to do civilian work essential to the war effort or registered to carry out non-combatant duties in the army. Many of the conscientious objectors simply said that they could not take human life, but most were willing to work in non-combatant roles. This was accepted and numbers of them were sent to the battle fronts where they worked as medical orderlies, drivers, auxiliaries, dispatch riders, mechanics, clerks, or in essential war work occupations such as mining, agriculture, forestry or hospitals.

The general reaction to conscientious objectors was roughly the same as in 1914-1918, many still labelled them cowards. However, to some extent, conscientious objectors who were willing to work hard and contribute to the war effort were tolerated. Some even became bomb disposal experts because they saw that as a way of saving lives. The main problems were caused by those who refused to undertake war work at all. While on the one hand it was felt that there should be choice, and that fighting should be an option rather than compulsory, on the other hand people were having to sacrifice their lives to preserve that freedom of choice, especially as Hitler was not noted for his tolerant liberalism. Employers refused to give them jobs and they were often shunned by everyone, family, friends and acquaintances.

As well as military conscription there was also what was termed 'industrial conscription'. From May 1940 onwards the Minister of Labour and National Service had had the authority to *'direct any person to perform such services which in the opinion of the Minister the person directed is capable of performing...'* This was so that essential industries, such as food provision, armaments, munitions, shipbuilding, aircraft manufacture, for example, would not suffer from labour shortages and be unable to fulfil their obligations. Also included were compulsory fire watching duties.

Christmas in 1941 was a muted affair. There was a great paper shortage so there were few Christmas decorations available commercially. Primary school children, like those at Fen Ditton School in Cambridgeshire, painted old newspapers and cut them in to strips which were then glued together and used to make paper chains. The Scouts undertook regular paper collections, but mothers and teachers tried to save just a few newspapers for the children. Attics were scoured for objects wrapped in old newspapers, plain paper or tissue paper. Wrapping paper was scarce to the point of unobtainability which meant keeping presents a surprise was difficult. No one wished to rob the war effort, but it was felt that the children deserved a little excitement. Most presents were home-made, and it was also considered patriotic to buy war bonds, National Savings certificates, or savings stamps books. Traditional Christmas food was also severely curtailed, but Cambridgeshire folk knew that they were not as deprived as some areas. The county was, however, painfully aware, that if the Germans repeated the Blitzkrieg of Christmas 1940, then geographically, they were right in the firing line. Watching their children play popular games like marbles or skipping and remembering their loved ones fighting at the fronts, those on the Home Front could only pray that somehow everything would turn out to be all right.

America Joins the War

The year did not begin well for Cambridgeshire. On 9 January an RAF B17 Flying Fortress crashed at Shepreth, while on a training flight, killing all its crew. These large planes, known as 'the Queen of the Skies', carried a full crew of ten including the pilot and co-pilot, a navigator and a bombardier, and half a dozen gunners, one of whom acted as engineer and another who acted as radio operator. The tables were finally turned in September, when a Dornier Do217, after bombing RAF Bourn as well as the University Farm in Girton, was shot down by a Mosquito night fighter and crashed near Orwell, killing all the German crew.

The so-called 'Baedecker Blitz' of April and May 1942 spooked the citizens of Cambridge even further because cultural and historical targets had been chosen as reprisals for the devastating RAF attacks on Lübeck and Rostock which had shocked many Germans. However, although Cambridge could not know this at the time, Hitler had expressly forbidden any attack on the university. Nevertheless, on 28 July, central Cambridge was attacked quite viciously and 137 buildings were hit (particularly on Round Church Street); three people were killed and seven were injured. There was considerable destruction and, it is fair to say, the fact the university was not hit was due more to good luck than good management. However, the city escaped comparatively lightly with 20 fatalities and 1,500 injuries during the course of the war. Nearby Newmarket, a small town on the Suffolk Cambridgeshire border, lost 30 of its citizens with many more injured, while London suffered some 40,000 casualties during the Blitz. The inhabitants of Cambridge and of the southern part of the county were awed and thoroughly unnerved by the constant orange glow in the night-time sky as London burned.

Consequently, the Starfish sites deemed necessary to protect the city of Cambridge were built at nearby Fulbourn in May 1942, which was categorised a 'temporary Starfish site', as were its supporting fellows at Babraham and Comberton. There was also a decoy site built in Coldham, four miles from Cambridge, for the Whitemoor railway yard. Boxworth and Rampton decoys were designed to protect RAF Oakington while Great Eversden and Horseheath Starfish sites protected RAF Duxford. Haddenham and Soham decoys protected

Fields of corn on remote farmland between the villages of Barton and Comberton cover the starfish decoy sites that protected Cambridge.

Waterbeach. However, most Starfish sites had been decommissioned by September 1943, after just fifteen months of use, mainly because, by this time, the Luftwaffe had recognised the decoy sites for what they were. Despite the nature of these Starfish sites, aerial photography reveals no trace of the Fulbourn site which has long since been reinstated for agricultural use. Babraham, Barton, Castle Camps and Comberton remain fairly remote rural villages with large swathes of cornfields and farmland. To date, few, if any, visible traces of the former Cambridgeshire Starfish sites have been detected.

In addition, out in the countryside of Cambridgeshire, armoured trains patrolled the railways. Tank locomotives, which were little protected, were 'sandwiched' between armoured trucks camouflaged to the point where they resembled railway engine tenders. Mostly manned by the Home Guard, the trains patrolled a triangular route: Cambridge – Hitchin – Bedford – Cambridge, protecting large numbers of wartime traffic trains. The LNER and LMS, both independent railway companies before nationalisation and on whose beat Cambridge lay, made necessary adjustments to accommodate all the extra activity. Coldham Lane junction, sidings and 'up goods yard' were extended; the 'hump yard' (where goods waggons were stacked and held for various destinations) was relocated and a water pump house at Chesterton Junction was built to expand the water supply for railway engines. Cambridge Goods Yard signal box was also rebuilt and extended to cope with the expansion of sidings at Long Road in Trumpington and extended staff facilities.

The GHQ Line

There was a lesser known, but equally important, reason why the Germans were so keen to bomb the railways around Cambridge and in Cambridgeshire. Although the county is landlocked, it is not far from the East Coast which was very vulnerable to attack during the war. The coast itself was quite well defended but there was also an inner line of defence known as the GHQ line. This line stretched from Highbridge, Somerset, in the west, to London and then turned north through Essex, Cambridgeshire, Norfolk, and continued up to Richmond in Yorkshire. Its purpose was to hinder any invasion force to allow time for military reinforcements to reach the area.

The line consisted of various obstacles including rivers, anti-tank ditches, tank traps, explosives and road blocks, which were guarded by pill boxes, gun emplacements and blockades; and the railways offered vital supply lines protected by the armoured trains. The GHQ line ran across Cambridgeshire and the city of Cambridge lay right on its path which ran through the city from the outlying villages of Great Chesterford and Stapleford on the Essex side, then on to Ely and Littleport and up to the Wash on the Norfolk side. Within the city itself the line crossed Hinton Way, Worts Causeway, and Queen Edith's Way, to run alongside Mowbray Road, crossing Cherry Hinton Road to run parallel with Perne Road, then, after crossing Birdwood Road, turning north-east to cross the two Newmarket railway lines, crossing Coldham's Lane and running along Keynes Road to Chesterton Junction before following the River Cam to Ely.

Much of the eastern side of Cambridge, which the line traversed, has been subject to extensive re-development and virtually no traces remain of the GHQ line's progress across the city. However, some scant remains of anti-tank ditches between the village of Stapleford and Wort's Causeway still exist, and out in the county of Cambridgeshire there are still a number of pillboxes dotted about the countryside. The GHQ line ran just to the east of the main north – south railway line through Cambridge, the line the Germans were so eager to destroy. Consequently, the area was heavily protected by tank ditches, road blocks and over forty pill boxes. One anti-tank ditch ran just north of Chesterton Junction

101 Cambs. Home Guard A.A. Battery, R.A. 1944. (Courtesy of Cambridge Local Studies)

round towards Huntingdon Road, while the other ran south of the city from near the junction of Madingley Road and Grange Road towards Grantchester. There were road blocks on Long Road near the Bedford railway line bridge; Hills Road railway bridge; Mill Road railway bridge; Coldham's Lane near the railway bridge; Newmarket Road railway bridge and Fen Road level crossing near Chesterton Junction.

Three of the pill boxes were situated at Chesterton Junction, Barnwell Junction and Coldham's Lane. These installations would have been manned by local Home Guard platoons, of which there were several in Cambridge, and there were many more in the county. Most towns and villages, for example: Ely, Willingham, Meldreth, Isleham and Girton had their own Local Defence Volunteers (LDV), more commonly known as the Home Guard, or 'Dad's Army', who were responsible for the initial defence of their localities in case of invasion, as well as their more general duties. The Home Guard mainly comprised men who were either too young or too old to enlist in the armed forces or had medical conditions which prevented them from serving in the army, navy or air force. A sizeable number of them were veterans of the last war who already had military training and expertise. They wore military uniform when on duty and took part in drills and training but most of them also had 'day jobs'. The portrayal of the Home Guard in 'Dad's Army' is said to be uncomfortably accurate at times, especially in reference to inadequate uniform and weaponry supplies, as well as having to contribute, sometimes substantially, out of their own pockets, towards Home Guard requirements. For example, one Home Guard platoon in Cambridgeshire was informed that if they wished to train on Sundays they must pay for a signalman's wages so that they could cross a local railway line. Those of the Home Guard directly responsible for guarding the railways in the city were located on Mill Road, Hills Road and Milton Road.

Royal visit Burwell Fen, 1942. (Courtesy of Cambridge Local Studies)

In May aircraft from RAF Bassingbourn, including twenty Wellington bombers, took part in the 'Thousand Bomber Raid' on Cologne, an exercise initiated by Sir Arthur Harris, Marshal of the Royal Air Force and Commander-in-Chief of Bomber Command. He was dubbed 'Bomber' Harris by the Press and 'Butcher Harris' by the RAF. Harris was a fan of 'strategic bombing' and 'area bombing' and he tended to be dismissive of the toll on his aircrews and the numbers of civilian deaths on the ground. He was also responsible for a week-long air raid on Hamburg in July 1943 which killed 43,000 people, many in a massive firestorm, injuring a further 37,000; and the raid on Dresden in February 1945, creating another firestorm which killed 25,000 people. Such raids were, he said, simply retribution for the Blitz on England, and, after Dresden, he wrote '... *attacks on cities...are strategically justified in so far as they tend to shorten the war and preserve the lives of Allied soldiers...I do not personally regard the whole of the remaining cities in Germany as worth the bones of one British Grenadier...*' King George VI must have found this view quite difficult since all his immediate family (with the exception of his Scottish wife and his Danish paternal grandmother, Queen Alexandra) were 100 per cent German (and had been since 1714), but his subjects were 100 per cent British.

The Yanks Arrive

This was the year that the Americans arrived on the English mainland in force, having joined the Allies and declared war on Germany and Japan as a result of the (to them) unprovoked bombing of Pearl Harbor. There were a number of American military installations established in Cambridgeshire, Suffolk and Norfolk. While the US Navy and US troops played a vital part in the war as well, the immediate impact on Cambridgeshire was the arrival of the US Airforce. Soon after the Americans came to East Anglia, an American regional base, American Army General Depot G-23 Histon, was established between Kings Hedges Road and Milton Road on the edge of Cambridge, not far from the St Ives (Hunts) railway line. In East Anglia most air force personnel came from the Eighth US Air Force, and some from the Ninth US Air Force, and they were located on around a hundred airbases within the region, forming a formidable fighting force.

The main aircraft in service with the US Air Force were the B-17 Flying Fortress and B-24 Liberator, both large planes, plus the P-51 Mustang, P-38 Lightning and P-47 Thunderbolt. The legendary 'Memphis Belle' was based at Bassingbourn airfield and 'Sally B' was located at Duxford. Both were Flying Fortresses,

Bassingbourn Airfield, Memphis Belle, 1940s.

their size and crew capacity of ten men justifying the type name of the plane, and they were chiefly used on bombing missions. The B-24 flew at lower altitudes than the B-17 and sustained more losses as a result. All the remaining three planes were used by Fighter Command. The P-47 Thunderbolt was the largest, deemed 'a flying tank,' it was nicknamed 'the Jug' (from the word Juggernaut), or, more unkindly, the 'Flying Milk Bottle', by the pilots who flew it. The P-38 Lightning was also a large aircraft which often acted as an escort to the bombers. The P-51 Mustang was a lighter plane which did not climb well, but which could dive very fast and efficiently, and was often used on reconnaissance missions. RAF Bottisham, RAF Fowlmere, RAF Molesworth, RAF Steeple Morden, as well as RAF Bassingbourn and RAF Duxford, became USAAF Cambridgeshire (what is now south and east of the larger post-war county) airfield bases during the war. Occasionally, RAF Mepal, the home of New Zealand No.75 Squadron, may also have hosted American planes.

RAF Bassingbourn was assigned as USAAF Designation Station 21 on 10 August 1942 (remaining so until 25 June 1945), serving as the headquarters for the 1st Combat Bombardment Wing of the 1st Bomb Division, and the RAF largely moved out. Large numbers of support resources were required and USAAF station units assigned to Bassingbourn included:

441st Sub-Depot (VIII Air Force Service Command)
18th Weather Squadron
1st Station Complement Squadron
Regular Army Station Units assigned to Bassingbourn included:
831st Engineer Aviation Battalion
204th Quartermaster Company
1696th Ordnance and Maintenance Supply Company
863rd Chemical Company (Air Operations)
982nd Military Police company
985th Military Police company
2024th Engineer Fire Fighting Platoon
206th Finance Section
3rd Mobile Training Unit
556th Army Postal Unit

On 13 October 1942 Bassingbourn's distribution of USAAF resources received the addition of the USAAF 91st Bombardment Group (Heavy) comprising:

322nd Bombardment Squadron
323rd Bombardment Squadron
324th Bombardment Squadron
401st Bombardment Squadron

In November these squadrons began a campaign of attacks on German submarines and their land-based manufacturing units.

The arrival of the American forces also had a considerable impact on the social scene of Cambridgeshire. Integration with the local people was generally welcomed by US servicemen far from home and sometimes lonely, and as a result, many friendships and several romances were formed. At the Eagle Hotel in Cambridge American airmen left their signatures on the pub walls and ceiling. The Americans brought with them the 'big band sound' (Glenn Miller was established in nearby Bedford), jitterbug dances, peanut butter, chewing gum, Coca Cola, and a host of other things. Cambridgeshire folk found that GIs from the local air bases seemed to have access to a plentiful supply of nylon stockings, chocolates and whisky which were not on ration in the United States. This mostly delighted Cambridgeshire women but considerably annoyed large numbers of local men who considered, along with many other Englishmen, that '...the Yanks were overpaid, over-sexed and over here...'

Ely Cathedral which helped organise the accommodation of the Kindertransport children.

Town and Gown

The war had somehow managed to divide Cambridgeshire into three distinct sections. The county, most of which was focused on the building and servicing of new airfields and decoy sites, caring for evacuees and growing food for the war effort. The city was mainly focused on receiving and accommodating refugees/evacuees, dealing with the bombing attacks and protecting its railway system. The university, which, for the first two years, had managed to carry on life almost as normal, was now forced to focus on loss of staff and students to military roles, reorganisation of its academic priorities and housing military personnel. Relations between town and gown had always been problematical. Whilst it was acknowledged that the university brought a good deal of business and money into the city, there was also a festering resentment that, because at this time male students greatly outnumbered female students, the male students, in search of female company, helped themselves to the town girls. Students, the 'gown boys', usually came from very different backgrounds to the town boys; many of them had more money and it became a badge of honour for a town girl to have a gown boyfriend. This, not unnaturally, caused problems and on the annual university 'rag days' the two sectors often clashed violently. By 1942, however, real life was catching up with the university. Both students and fellows were being called up and numbers had reduced to around three fifths of normal.

Alan Turing, a young and gifted mathematician, the 'father of computing', was a Fellow of King's College and when the war began he had been called up to Bletchley Park to join their team of cypher code breakers. Here, he was involved in one of the most significant and important developments of the entire war, which took place in 1941, but it would be over thirty years before any information about it was released. Alan Turing pioneered the breaking of the Enigma code at Bletchley Park, the top-secret government codebreaking and crypto-analysis headquarters. During the 1930s the Germans had developed Enigma machines used for sending coded messages, initially on German security issues. Shortly before the outbreak of war, the Polish Cypher Bureau, at the Warsaw Conference in July 1939, gave British and French intelligence officers the basic details of the construction and working of German Enigma machines as well as their methods of decryption. The Polish method, however, did not cope well with the Germans' changing procedures or details. Turing took a more general approach based on decryption for breaking the codes. Working in the now legendary Hut 8 he developed indicator procedures which could break the codes used by the German army. The naval Enigma codes had much more complicated indicator systems that were difficult to decipher. Turing worked on this alone at first and eventually solved problems by his use of 'sequential analysis' in the summer of 1941. His work was said to have shortened the war by two years, although no-one knew it at the time, but in 1946 he was awarded the OBE for his work in helping to break the cypher code of the Enigma machine.

Honours were also bestowed on economist John Maynard Keynes, a Fellow of King's, who was a senior economic advisor to the Treasury during both world wars where his economic policies were both pertinent and eminently workable. The loss of academic staff and a reduction in professorships had an impact on teaching within the university and the loss of students had an impact on general university numbers. Although arts faculties were reducing, it was felt that, as America had now joined the war, the university should honour this by establishing a chair of American History. This had been officially proposed by the Vice Chancellor of St John's in his 1941 review and the election of the first postholder was subsequently confirmed in 1943, although by 1942 only 143 of the original 370 university lecturers and demonstrators remained in the university.

The effect of this war was not as dramatic as during the First World War just over twenty years previously and government funding had remained adequate. Civil Defence and the Home Guard had also placed additional burdens on remaining staff, but by this time, the university had initiated a scheme whereby students could come to Cambridge as military cadets and spend two terms reading the subject of their choice while doing their military training. These two terms and passing their cadet examinations would contribute to a special war degree if they returned to the university after the war to complete their studies. Those not called up for military service, like the rest of the country, took their turn at fire-watching duties and 'digging for victory'. King's College had to suspend its daily choral services owing to a lack of choristers, but its annual carol services were maintained, although the Christmas Eve service of 1940 was held against a background accompaniment of aeroplanes flying into battle overhead.

University social activities, as in many other places, were severely restricted by the wartime conditions and privations. There was, however, still a whiff of unreality around. In 1941 King's College had celebrated the 500th anniversary of its foundation in 1441 and, although many of the planned celebrations were cancelled, the Ministry of Food had allowed the college to hold a 'feast of swan'. Normally only the sovereign is allowed to eat swan, although St John's College has a special agreement that swan may be served at its quinquennial May Ball. The college servants must have looked at this 'feast' as they served it and thought of their own war-time meat rations, wondering why such indulgence was allowed when they, their families, and everyone else, had to make do with extremely scant rations.

The university colleges used any spare room they had as a result of reduced staff and student numbers to offer accommodation to academic evacuees and the armed forces. Queen Mary College in London and the LSE took advantage and so too did the RAF. The academic evacuees appeared to fit fairly unobtrusively into university life but there seemed to be a good deal of friction with the RAF and complaints on both sides were common. The colleges complained about noise, the lack of staff to cope with extra housekeeping duties, military vehicles parked within their grounds and general lack of consideration. The RAF in turn complained about room rates, the supply of sausages, cleaning toilets and china mugs. Just before Christmas in 1941 the squadron leader in charge of the RAF No.2 MT Company billeted at King's College, had written a sniffy letter to the college bursar stating that, owing to breakages, there were insufficient china mugs for the use of the airmen and insisting upon priority and urgency of supply by the college in ordering replacement china mugs. History does not appear to have recorded the bursar's reply.

The Cambridgeshire Regiment

At the beginning of 1942 the 1st Battalion of the Cambridgeshire Regiment fought at the Battle of Sime Road Camp, the RAF headquarters for Malaya in Singapore, but were forced to surrender to the Imperial Japanese Army. Meanwhile the 2nd Battalion of the Cambridgeshire Regiment had arrived in Singapore early in 1942 to assist the 15th Indian Brigade at Batu Pahat, although they too finally had to surrender to the Japanese, suffering even heavier losses than the 1st Battalion. Sime Road Camp subsequently became a Japanese internment camp for PoWs. After Singapore had fallen to the Japanese Army most of the prisoners were initially interned in work camps like Sime Road, but at the end of 1942 they were sent to work on the infamous Thai-Burmese Railway.

However, it was in the summer of 1942 that El Alamein, a small Egyptian town and railway halt on the Mediterranean coast, entered the general consciousness of the British public, and this would finally give some cheerful news. The First Battle of El Alamein (1-27 July) had been fought in Egypt between the Afrika Korps of the Axis forces commanded by Field Marshal Erwin Rommel (the Desert Fox) and the Eighth Army of the Allied forces commanded by General (later Field Marshal) Claude Auchinleck. The Axis forces were coming dangerously close to the cities and ports of Egypt, but the Allies had so far managed to prevent further advances. The Second Battle of El Alamein (23 October – 11 November) took place with Lieutenant General Bernard Montgomery (Monty as he became

Cambridgeshire Regiment on Parade, 1946. (Courtesy of Cambridge Local Studies)

affectionately known) replacing General Auchinleck as commander of the Allied Forces. Monty's eventual victory at El Alamein was a turning point in the war. The resulting victory for the Allies ended the Axis threat to Egypt and the Suez Canal, as well as to the Persian and Middle Eastern oilfields, and marked a turning point in the North Africa campaign.

Down on the Farm

Farming was having its usual tough time and the Ministry of Agriculture felt that the harvest of 1942 could well be critical for the country. Farmers were also being asked to give detailed crop plans for 1943. The fertile soils of Cambridgeshire were good for crops, especially wheat (the War Agriculture Committee had asked that standard red wheat be grown for the war effort because it had a high protein content), potatoes, onions, carrots, celery, sugar beet, and the mangel wurzels used for winter animal feed. Hay was also important for animal fodder. Haystacks were still common because combine harvesters and baling were not in general use until after the war. Although many farms had the use of basic tractors due to the shortage of horses after the First World War, the economic depression of the 1930s had prevented much investment in buying farm machinery.

There were different styles of hay-rick but they had to be built so that they did not topple over and in such a manner that they did not catch fire in a hot sun. Hay is the leaf and seed material of cut grasses while straw comprises the stems which contain less nutrition for the animals. Rain causes rot and mould in hay, so it was important to try and cut the hay when it was sunny and the grasses were dry. Afterwards the ricks would be covered, or sometimes thatched with straw. It was important at haymaking time that everyone pitched in to help and even children as young as five were expected to assist.

Many farms kept at least a few cows for milk and butter and cheese. Waste materials from cheese and butter making could be fed to pigs, along with other scraps, and during the war people were encouraged to keep a pig for bacon, ham and pork. Some of the towns had pig clubs where a number of people would club together and buy a pig which would be kept wherever there was room for it. When the fattened pig was killed, everyone who had shares in the pig could receive some extra bacon and ham after the Ministry of Food had taken its requisitioned share. This was a double-edged sword, however, as those who received their share of a pig were not allowed other meat rations until they had eaten all of the meat allocated from the pig. In the Cambridgeshire countryside there were also plenty of rabbits and these were not rationed. However, rabbit is quite a strong-tasting meat, too strong for most modern tastes, and even during wartime conditions there were those who simply could not face a daily dose of rabbit stew.

Many Cambridgeshire farms lacked the amenities or 'mod cons' taken for granted in the twenty-first century. There were still no supplies of mains gas, electricity, or water, and no mains sewage system, for many of the more remote country hamlets and farm labourers' cottages. Cooking was mostly either done on a primus stove or using calor gas, while some of the larger farm kitchens had an Aga which was usually kept burning day and night. Water came from rain butts or wells and light was provided by oil, paraffin and Tilley lamps. Toilets were either Elsan-type (chemical) or in the form of slop buckets which had to be emptied daily and the contents carefully buried.

These conditions of comparative simplicity were not a result of the war. It was just how life was and there had not been much progress towards more modern times. The contrast with living conditions in the city of Cambridge was decidedly marked. Even as late as the 1950s some country folk continued to get up with the sun and go to bed with the sun. Poultry farming had declined generally but, during the First World War fresh eggs had generally been more freely available and in the Eastern Counties there had been concerted efforts to expand and promote the poultry industry. However, although meeting with some success, keeping hens generally continued to remain what it had always been, more of a cottage industry. The inevitable result was that when war came there was an acute shortage of eggs once again. Many Cambridgeshire farmers, however, cannily bought up as many hens as they could to produce extra eggs, which resulted in local surplus production. Despite this, however, farmers and their families were not allowed more than the official egg ration of one egg per week (although enforcing this rule was virtually impossible) and surplus eggs had to be preserved in water glass (a solution of sodium or potassium silicate).

The absence of fresh eggs was partly compensated by dried eggs, the subject of the most frequent complaints about food during the war. Dried egg powder was imported from America and made up with water. One tin was usually the equivalent of a dozen fresh eggs. It was used in cake mixes or recipes where the taste was disguised but its use for scrambled eggs, omelettes, or in egg-based sandwich spreads, was often disliked, and the one fresh egg a week which was allowed was much treasured. Government attempts to extoll the virtues of dried eggs fell on deaf ears and many people simply preferred to go without them. Research and fieldwork are always a necessary part of writing history, so it was decided by the writer that dried eggs should be personally tested as they appeared to have been so disliked. Dried egg powder is very fine and yellow with the consistency of a coarse custard powder and there is a faintly fishy smell when the packet is first opened. Made up with the requisite amount of water, it looks like a thin yellow custard sauce. However, once cooked (scrambled eggs were the choice of presentation) there was little to distinguish them from the real thing. Perhaps they are not quite so fluffy as fresh scrambled eggs, but the taste was the same as fresh eggs, although the texture was heavier. Obviously dried eggs could not be boiled or fried, but as scrambled eggs or an omelette there appears to be little real difference. However, it must be remembered that modern preserving and dehydration methods are much more sophisticated than eighty years ago, and today people are also far more used to reconstituted foods.

Once again there had been a threatened shortage of agricultural labourers as men were conscripted but the Women's Land Army (WLA) was working hard to make up the shortfall. The WLA was founded in the First World War and had proved that women were just as capable as men at carrying out farm work, so there was much less initial prejudice and resistance from farmers in the Second World War towards young women replacing men on their farms. In Cambridgeshire farmers' wives and daughters had done farm work for years anyway. The Land Army girls proved themselves to be quick learners and hard workers, and they were generally respected by the men with whom they worked. At first women

Thriplow Land Army Girls c1943. (Courtesy of Cambridge Local Studies)

volunteered to work in the WLA, but after the National Service Act was passed in 1941, women were called up for war work and had to choose between working in industry, the armed forces, teaching or the WLA. The Land Girls, as they were known, received minimal training and worked a minimum fifty-hour week, in all weathers, doing a variety of tasks which included milking, lambing, looking after sheep, chickens and other animals, ploughing, harvesting, digging ditches, catching rats and general farm maintenance work.

There was also a Timber Corps for chopping trees and running sawmills. The girls wore a uniform of green jumpers, brown trousers, khaki overcoats and brown hats. They lived either in hostels or on the farms where they worked. During the spring of 1940 agricultural workers had been awarded a minimum weekly wage of 48s (£120 in today's values) which, while low by modern standards, was a great improvement and an incentive for working on the land, but WLA members only received a fraction of these wages. Although the war ended in 1945 the WLA was not disbanded until 1950.

Food Facts

Food rationing was, at times, hard to bear, but, as in the latter part of the First World War, the general health of the nation was reasonably robust in that everyone was receiving, in roughly equal shares, something of everything.

Vegetarians could hand in their meat and bacon coupons for which they received double cheese rations and two eggs per week. Diabetics had to surrender their sugar coupons. Three pints of milk (1.70 litres) were allocated per person per week and one tin of milk powder (eight pints or 4.5 litres) every eight weeks. Expectant mothers, children and invalids were given priority and often received extra milk rations. There were some special extra rations for certain civilian jobs which included heavy physical labour, including mine workers, farm and forestry workers, the Women's Land Army, land drainage workers and railway transport personnel (except dining car staff).

Men need an average basic calorie allowance of 2,500 calories per day, whereas women only need 2,000. In civilian life this was reflected within the rations allowed reasonably fairly, but in the Army and the Merchant Navy, there appeared to have been some quite severe discrimination. Armed forces personnel could not be judged by the standards of a civilian population but there were marked disparities between male and female allocations. Men were allowed double the amount of meat, sugar and tea, a third more jam and syrup, and 25 per cent more butter or margarine than women; in addition to which women were only allowed margarine but strictly no butter. The only concession to women was that they were allowed one ounce (28g) more bacon than men.

Fish and chips, so long a British staple meal, were also scarce. Fish was very expensive due to the risk and manpower involved in obtaining it, especially as German submarines were active around British coasts trying to sink as much merchant shipping as they could. Cambridgeshire was near enough to the Norfolk coast, but so too were the U-boats. The inland waterways, of which the county had more than its share, supported some freshwater fish, but Cambridgeshire folk, along with the rest of the British people, were used to their traditional deep-sea fish of cod, plaice and haddock. Snoek, a South African fish, and whale meat were imported and promoted as alternative sources of fish, but most of the British fell back onto their traditionally conservative approach to food and refused to eat what they suspiciously termed 'foreign fish', preferring to go without whale meat as it was too tough and Snoek because 'it tasted too fishy'! Chips, however, were plentiful but, due to the very inferior fats used to fry them in wartime, many found them rather unpalatable.

The 'black market' was causing problems. This involved any unofficial trade in rationed goods such as food, clothing or fuel, and those found guilty could face a fine of £500 (over £20,000 at 2018 values) plus up to two years imprisonment. The rewards were such, however, that a fair number took the chance. Nationally, farmers and smallholders were found to be the main culprits in producing food for the black market, often from surplus stocks. One MP described the black market as *'treason of the very worst kind'*. Another called for black marketeers to be whipped with a 'cat o' nine tails' before being sent to do long term penal servitude or hard labour. There is, however, no real evidence to show that Cambridgeshire farming people were involved in the black market, and, with many living in small, often isolated, communities, they were far more likely to have shared any surplus food with family and friends than selling it at a great profit on the black market.

Cambridgeshire, especially the city, was far more concerned about the rapidly rising crime rate. Crimes ranged from looting, theft, burglary and fraud to assault, rape and murder. There was looting from businesses damaged in air raids and bombed houses, abuse of government-funded compensation schemes, and instances of trying to charge people entry fees to air raid shelters; although these crimes were usually confined to the city. Mercifully, murder was fairly rare, but assaults and rape became far more common. Punishments could be severe. Young offenders were often birched while older ones received lengthy terms of hard labour. Rape was the most difficult crime to prove. There were rarely witnesses and it was a case of the victim's word against that of the perpetrator. Cover of darkness was a rapist's friend, making any attempt at initial defence against the perpetrator difficult and also making it easy for them to escape. If they were unknown to the victim, the police would have little to go on and any defence lawyer would accuse victims of making it all up so as to hide the fact that they were girls 'of easy virtue'. Unwanted pregnancy could ruin a girl's life but, in the days before DNA testing, all a man had to do was to deny paternity. Unfortunately, as in the First World War, public and legal sympathy tended to lie with the male and many cases of rape went unreported. Cambridgeshire's real strength and protection against physical assaults was the number of small communities where everyone knew everyone else and culprits could be much more easily apprehended.

In March it was announced that civilian petrol rations would be abolished on 1 July and this greatly affected rural areas. From July petrol was only allowed to be used by the armed forces, the emergency services, bus companies and farmers (for machinery and transport of commodities). Fuel approved for official use contained red dye to confirm authenticity and so that misappropriated stocks could be easily traced. Inappropriate use of petrol became a criminal offence. There was consequently a great deal of protest and the Welsh actor/composer, Ivor Novello, received a penalty of four weeks imprisonment for misappropriation and misuse of petrol coupons.

The Beveridge Report

The government remained keenly aware of the fact that British society was far from equal. There had been no 'land fit for heroes' after the last war, only another two decades of austerity, and this was causing severe problems for millions of people who had already given all of what little they had. There was also a strong perception that the wealthier sections of society were not paying their fair share. In an attempt to address the problems, and to keep low income workers and the poorer sections of society on side, Sir William Beveridge had been commissioned to write a report proposing the beginnings of a social security system. This report was published on 1 December and its basis was to '*introduce a system of social insurance from cradle to grave*'. Beveridge believed that all workers should pay a weekly contribution which would then be paid back in benefits to cover sickness, unemployment, retirement or being widowed. The main points of his report were:

- *"Proposals for the future should not be limited by "sectional interests" in learning from experience and that a "revolutionary moment in the world's history is a time for revolutions, not for patching".*
- *Social insurance is only one part of a "comprehensive policy of social progress". The five giants on the road to reconstruction were Want, Disease, Ignorance, Squalor and Idleness.*
- *Policies of social security "must be achieved by co-operation between the State and the individual", with the state securing the service and contributions. The state "should not stifle incentive, opportunity, responsibility; in establishing a national minimum, it should leave room and encouragement for voluntary action by each individual to provide more than that minimum for himself and his family".*

There was already free hospital treatment available for war casualties, but this was laying the groundwork for the introduction of a National Health Service and Beveridge argued, against much opposition, that the recommendations in his report would also provide a minimum standard of living. To guarantee this aim a minimum wage was needed, which had long been the ultimate dream of workers, trades unionists and strikers. However, many in the middle and upper classes still felt this might encourage fecklessness and recklessness among the working classes, but the *Manchester Guardian* called the report '*a big and fine thing,*' while the *Daily Telegraph* said that it was '*a consummation of the revolution begun by David Lloyd George in 1911*'. The Archbishop of Canterbury declared that it was *'the first time anyone had set out to embody the whole body of the Christian spirit in an Act of Parliament'.*

It was a revolutionary concept which represented the beginnings of a more enlightened and compassionate attitude towards social welfare. Since the beginning of the Industrial Revolution, and before, it had been the practice among the upper classes to lay the blame for poverty and unemployment on the poor themselves. The idea of a fair day's pay for a fair day's work was a relatively new concept, since, in Victorian England the aim had generally been to keep wages as low as possible on the grounds of efficiency and economy. This had certainly been the case for agricultural workers for centuries and Cambridgeshire folk welcomed the new proposals warmly but quietly. Many in the countryside still lived in tied cottages and felt they owed at least some superficial loyalty to their landlords. The upper classes, however, felt that the need to work for long hours just to earn enough for food and shelter should inspire folk to work hard rather than having to increase the costs of production by paying higher wages and thus encourage the idleness which might result. However, low wages and rising prices meant in many cases that workers 'had to run just to stand still'. It was time for change. Churchill was lukewarm about the whole thing (he would subsequently vote against the foundation of a National Health Service), but he agreed in principle, although he warned that these reforms would have to wait until the end of the war before they could be implemented.

A severe shortage of timber was making matters difficult for companies manufacturing furniture. National demand for new furniture had been heavy in the wake of the Blitz and random bombings. Consequently, a Utility Furniture Advisory Committee had been established in 1941 and it was decided to ration new furniture to newly-weds and those who had lost their homes through bombing. The Domestic Furniture (Control of Manufacture and Supply) Order became operative in November 1942. There were a number of approved furniture designs and a catalogue was published early in 1943. Designs were simple and unadorned in the style of the Arts and Crafts Movement. Items were basic and functional. The same logo, 'CC41', was used for utility furniture as had been used for utility clothing, and the two commodities became known as 'the two cheeses'.

GIs at Christmas

From the other side of the globe, by Christmas time this year, there were over 60,000 American GIs in Britain including a number of black servicemen. This fact seemed to bother the white GIs far more than it bothered the population of their host country and there were a number of racist incidents. During these incidents, however, it was noted that English people would generally defend the black GIs. Although unused to seeing black men in service uniforms, it wasn't as though Cambridgeshire had never seen a black person and they welcomed GIs regardless of colour or creed. The main problem with the GIs, many Englishmen decided, jealous of the treats no longer available in Britain which the Americans could provide, was that they had arrived rather late and missed much of the real action. In turn some of the Americans regarded Britain as a *'quaint, shabby, rather backward country with obsessions of class differentiation and tea drinking'*.

The authorities, in attempting to make relations more cordial and improve social integration, suggested that, as the GIs were far from home, it would be nice if British families would invite them to spend Christmas Day in their homes. They would not be expected to feed them from their own meagre rations as each GI would be issued with a provision pack for his or her hosts. These included spam, coffee, biscuits, cake, chocolate, tinned peaches and soups. They also brought presents of nylons, chocolates, whisky and cigarettes, commodities mostly no longer available in Britain, with chewing gum and comics for the children.

Initially the British were overwhelmed but a little wary. The film, *Yanks*, made by John Schlesinger in the 1970s, has a scene in which a young GI spends Christmas Day with his English girlfriend's family. His girlfriend's mother unwraps his gift to her of a Christmas cake painfully slowly, undoing the string and winding it into a ball, then carefully folding the wrapping paper, before she finally lifts the lid of the box to reveal the cake. She is astonished at seeing such a rich cake and what she believes is so much ostentation. She acknowledges her thanks to him very briefly before carefully replacing the cake in its box, and, with the lid firmly back in place, puts it aside. It is probably an uncomfortably accurate depiction of many first such meetings, but it was not all bad. The GIs told their hosts about their families and Christmas at home, of the Christmas customs of advent calendars and hanging ginger biscuits on the Christmas tree. Their British hosts swapped tales and explained about Christmas crackers which many GIs had not seen before. Most of the American air bases were in the East Anglian counties, and so having a GI to Christmas dinner in Cambridgeshire was not uncommon.

The year ended for Cambridgeshire on a rather more positive, if slightly humorous, note. 'Careless talk costs lives' thundered the war propaganda posters; the government clearly anxious that any German spies who had infiltrated the country and its institutions should learn nothing of value. Nine days before

Christmas, a German spy with the very English name of Eddie Chapman parachuted from a German aircraft and landed near Littleport. He happily gave himself up to the police not realising that they knew who he was and that they also knew that he was on a spying mission for the Germans to learn whatever he could, mostly just by chatting to people. When he realised that he'd destroyed his own objectives, he eventually turned and became a double agent, one of whose main achievements would be to report to the Germans incorrectly playing down the efficiency and accuracy of V1s, better known as doodlebugs.

The Bevin Boys, Conscription of Women and GIs Help Out

The Minister of Labour, Ernest Bevin, as leader of the TGWU, had suffered severe embarrassment over strikes in the transport industry. By the middle of 1943 the mining industry was short staffed and in desperate need of 40,000 miners. Coal production had slumped and by December Britain had just three weeks' supply of coal in reserve. Voluntary requests for new miners had made little impact so Ernest Bevin introduced a scheme whereby a proportion of conscripted men would work in the mines instead of being drafted into the armed forces. This was done by means of a ballot. As a result, 48,000 'Bevin Boys' were sent to work down the mines. Half had been selected by ballot, which denied any choice of serving in the armed forces, and half were volunteers who preferred mining to the armed forces. The ballot was simple. Every month a number was drawn from a hat. All men whose National Service Registration Number ended with the same number were sent down the mines. Refusal to accept could mean a fine or imprisonment.

The 'Bevin Boys' were sent to work in the various coal mines of England, Wales and Scotland, and represented about 10 per cent of those aged 18-25 called up during the last two years of the war. This caused a great deal of resentment, and especially for young lads who had dreamed of honour in the armed services it was a bitter disappointment. There was also the added frustration of misunderstanding by the public. Mining was a vital necessity to the war, but many saw it as an opt-out from combatant service, although anyone who had ever been down a coal mine knew otherwise. Mining conscripts came from all classes and all regions. There were a number of government training centres, mostly in England, where they received a basic six weeks of training before being sent down the mines. Conscripts usually lived in Nissan huts adjacent to the mines where they worked. The initial experience of descending hundreds of feet below ground to work in the cramped, silent, airless, twilight of middle earth must have been terrifying, especially for those who suffered from claustrophobia. Most worked with the pit ponies or on the conveyor belts alongside more experienced men but some worked at the coal face.

The National Coal Mining Museum has preserved a coal mine which the public can visit to experience how miners lived and worked. It is a terrifying learning curve which renders the word 'respect' quite inadequate. About twenty people are crammed into a wire cage measuring little more than 6ft (180cm) x 4ft (120cm) which descends jerkily 550ft (around 170m) down into the earth. There is no electric light. Each person is given a miner's lamp which is the only illumination. Cameras, phones and watches have to be left at the surface. It is dark, dirty, dank, damp and smells incredibly musty. Water drips down the walls of the shaft. Once in the mine there are lots of long narrow passages in which it is impossible for people over 5ft (150cm) tall to stand upright. At the coal face miners often had to sit or crouch to work the coal from the rock. Battered wooden doors were kept closed between each section to minimise the spread of fire risk. The rock presses in on all sides. Air quality sometimes fluctuates which can leave one hot and breathless with a pounding heart. Pneumoconiosis (known as 'black lung' by miners) is a dust-based lung disease, which was an occupational and fatal hazard for miners.

At this time there were few mechanical aids and it is an understatement to say that the work was hard, dangerous and unrelenting, for both men and animals. When pit ponies were used, they spent most of their time underground with just a few rest days, particularly the bank holidays, above ground. In the mine, small stalls were cut into the rock for them to be tethered when resting. There was a stone trough at one end and just sufficient room for the horse not to have to stand upright all the time. Many of them died below ground. The prospect of working down a mine was not attractive but it was necessary and essential war work.

Women's Rights

In the House of Commons Dr Edith Summerskill led a call for equal pay for women. She stated that in the auxiliary services women were replacing men 'head for head' but, although men were asking and obtaining the going rate for the jobs, women were paid well below that rate, at only two thirds of the rate which the men received. Yet members of the ATS worked as dispatchers, electricians, motor mechanics and cyclists; those in the WRNS did clerical work, despatch riding, wireless work and motor transport; women in the WAAF worked as wireless mechanics, electricians, aircraft hands and armament assistants. In addition, it was suggested that there should be a special wartime domestic corps for women with its own uniform. This would have suited Cambridgeshire women well. Dr Summerskill also said arguments put to her that women would deprive men of jobs in a competitive labour market were rubbish. Surely, she said, it was efficiency, not sex, which should be the benchmark.

The calling up of women in the 45-50 age group was criticised as well, when it was felt that there were younger women who could be called upon, but the government had in mind nursing, midwifery and hospital services which required older women with more experience. This raised further protests that jobs seen as 'women's work' were traditionally low paid which was why there was now a shortage of midwives, nurses, teachers and servants. As a result a number of MPs insisted that the government had a duty to revise pay and working conditions for women and that there should be equal pay for equal jobs and, furthermore, public opinion supported this view.

Britain managed to totally mobilise its population, both male and female, during the war. Like the First World War twenty years before, it was seen as a *'people's war that enlarged domestic aspirations and produced promises of a post-war welfare state'*. Back then women had kept the home fires burning and carried out the men's jobs while they were away as well as supplying the soldiers and sailors with 'comforts' (clothes, food, tobacco, books etc) and in doing so had gained the vote for themselves, much more independence, and the promise

The only ATS band in the country, Cambridge 1943. (Courtesy of Cambridge Local Studies)

of 'a land fit for heroes' to which their husbands could return. The 'land fit for heroes' did not materialise but now people believed that their efforts in this war would gain them a welfare state with adequate housing, education, social benefits and healthcare for all. This was why Britain had been so successful in mobilising its home front and much of this success was again due to the mobilisation of its women. In addition to paid work and conscription work, the country's women had once again supported the war effort, ensured that the rationing of food and clothing was successful, cared for their children, often on their own while the father was serving overseas, run the communal British restaurants, carried on the 'make do and mend' tradition and spearheaded conservation drives for paper, metal and bones.

Dark Days for the RAF

On the aerial missions front the first half of the year was fairly quiet, but this was not to last. In mid-July ten Messerschmidt Me 410s carried out a low-level bombing attack on the Cambridge and Waterbeach airfields. In November 115 Squadron moved to RAF Witchford where they gained the unhappy reputation of losing more aircraft in the war than any other RAF squadron. On 9 November there was a tragic accident near the remote and little used railway station of Shippea Hill not far from Ely. There was a mid-air collision resulting in a fatal crash. A Hercules Mk VI was flying with a Hurricane on an 'affiliation exercise'. The Hurricane got too close to the Hercules and snapped off a sizeable section of its wing. Both planes then crashed at Shippea Hill killing the pilot of the Hurricane and nine crew members of the Hercules. It was not a good time for the RAF in Cambridgeshire and worse was to come.

RAF Bourn, originally built as back-up to RAF Oakington, had grown by 1942 to become a bomber station with three runways but by this point in the war it had lost 135 planes, including 60 Lancaster bombers, 19 Wellington bombers, 24 Mosquito fighter-bombers and a considerable number of air crew. Lancaster bombers had carried out the daring and successful Dambusters raids of Operation Chastise in May of 1943.

However, on the night of 16/17 December RAF Bourn suffered a terrible tragedy on one of the worst nights on record for Bomber Command. No.97 Squadron (RAF) had arrived in April with their fleet of Lancasters and a large detachment of planes from the squadron left on a bombing mission to Berlin. Casualties from the mission itself were low but on their return to RAF Bourn the air crews discovered that thick fog had set in. Some planes diverted to Norfolk and Lincolnshire where they made safe landings. Others, however, decided to wait it out and the inevitable happened – their fuel ran out. As a result, eight aircraft: JB531 'OF-Y', JA963 'Q', JB243 'P', JB482 'S', JB219 'R', JB117 'C', JB119 'F' and JB176 'K' all crashed in the fog covering the airfield, killing most of their crews. The noise, the crashes and the resulting chaos around the airfield that night was described as unbelievable by locals. It was the most dreadful tragedy and the date passed into legend, becoming known as 'Black Thursday'. Like many Second World War airfields, RAF Bourn is now little more than a ghost. Some of the runways still remain, and one of two of the buildings, but much of the site has fallen victim to developers.

RAF Bottisham had a rather happier history, not difficult given the tragedies RAF Bourn had suffered. The Bottisham airfield opened in 1940 and was initially used by de Havilland Tiger Moths training on anti-invasion measures. The Tiger Moths left in 1941 and a number of RAF squadrons, including Nos.2, 4 169, 268, 288, 613 and 654, used the airfield until it was handed over to the USAAF in 1943. It was known as Station 374 and had the usual complement of support squadrons and companies, namely:

50th Service Group (VIII Air Force Command)
468th and 469th Service Squadrons
HHS 50th Service Group
18th Weather Squadron
66th Complement Squadron
1073rd Quartermaster Company
1097th Signal Company
1184th Military Police company
1598th Ordnance Supply and Maintenance Company
2118th Engineer Fire Fighting Platoon

The airfield was home to the 361st Fighter Group comprising the USAAF 374th, 375th and 376th Fighter Squadrons under the command of the 65th Fighter Wing of the VIII Fighter Command. The 361st Fighter Group's primary duties were escorting B-17 Flying Fortresses and Consolidated B-24 Liberators on bombing missions attacking various targets, but they undertook air patrols and dive-bombing activities as well. The group also took part in the D-Day operations. The weight of the heavy fighter planes took their toll on the soft, often wet, surface of Bottisham Airfield, frequently making take-off difficult, and in 1944 a temporary runway was laid out using steel matting.

By now the Americans had been in Britain for over a year and were well established, sharing several Cambridgeshire airfields with the RAF. They brought with them plane power and pilot power and were instrumental in helping the RAF keep the Luftwaffe firmly on the defensive. They also brought warships with them which greatly reduced Allied shipping losses. During 1942 800,000 tons of shipping had been lost, but by May 1943 the balance was being redressed with the sinking of 41 of the German fleet's 240 U-boats. This in turn reduced shipping losses by over half to less than 300,000 tons. It was an important step forward towards victory.

Almost two million American servicemen and women came to Britain to military bases and training camps especially established for that purpose. From Britain they could strike at the heart of the German war machine. The 350th Fighter Group of the USAAF had been operational at RAF Duxford from 1 October 1942 and RAF Duxford was subsequently allocated to the Eighth Airforce Fighter Command and was known as Station 357. USAAF station units also allocated to the base included:

79th Service Group 4
84th Service Squadron
378th Service Squadron

Duxford hand over to USAAF 1943. (Courtesy of Cambridge Local Studies)

HHS 79th Service Group
18th Weather Squadron
23rd Station Complement Squadron
1042nd Signal Company
1099th Quartermaster Company
1671st Ordnance Supply and Maintenance Company
989th Military Police Company
2027th Engineer Fire Fighting Platoon

In July 1943 the Fifth Air Defence Wing also arrived but transferred to Sawston Hall in August with a new name of 66th Fighter Wing. The Boeing B-17 Flying Fortress, including the legendary 'Memphis Belle', and the Consolidated B-24 Liberator bombers became common sights. John Steinbeck, the noted journalist and novelist, wrote newspaper articles on Bassingbourn during the spring and summer of 1943 as the Americans moved in and established themselves. The actor, Clark Gable, renowned for his part as Rhett Butler in *Gone with the Wind*, trained as a gunner with the USAAF and flew on missions in B-17 Flying Fortresses. He made a film, partly based on Bassingbourn, to recruit aerial gunners for the USAAF before he returned to the States.

Hospitals and Health

The county did not have a large number of hospitals during the Second World War. Addenbrooke's University Hospital in Cambridge was the largest general hospital. The RAF Hospital in Ely (now the Princess of Wales Hospital) specialised in treatments for burns. Papworth Hospital, although currently renowned for heart transplants, lung and liver surgery, was originally dedicated to the treatment of tuberculosis and during the war dealt with chest infections and respiratory complaints. Medical resources had improved since the last war and there was not the same need for the huge, often desperately under-staffed and under-supplied, field hospitals that trench warfare had necessitated.

There had been advancements in the discovery and testing of new drugs and their uses. Treatments were available in the Second World War which had been lacking in the first. Chief among these were Sulfanilamide, Penicillin, Atabrine, plasma and morphine. Sulfanilamide had been discovered in the 1930s by a German doctor and destroyed deadly streptococcal bacterial infections as well as combatting meningitis and pneumonia. Penicillin was also mass produced because of its effectiveness against wound infections, which, if left untreated, could turn gangrenous. Atabrine was used as a malarial treatment to replace dwindling quinine stocks. Plasma, a constituent of blood containing platelets, white blood cells and clotting agents, often replaced whole blood transfusions because it has a much longer storage life than blood. Morphine, derived from opium, is a powerful painkiller which was widely used and often carried in kit by soldiers, but, unfortunately, it also possesses addictive qualities.

By 1943 extra medical facilities were required for USAAF servicemen so the Army requisitioned land from Wimpole Hall to build a hospital to deal with casualties expected from an invasion of Europe and the Normandy landings planned for D-Day. Known as the 163 General Hospital, it was situated between USAAF Bassingbourn and Meldreth railway station, and not far from USAAF Fowlmere and RAF/USAAF Duxford. It was a good central point for the treatment of American casualties and wounded pilots, but it was, however, essentially a US military hospital, under US military control and it did not close its doors until early in 1946.

Christmas in Cambridgeshire in 1943 was a very make do and mend affair like most other places in the country. Virtually all presents were now home-made and there was still an acute shortage of paper. There were almost no chickens or geese available, a bit of pork if people were lucky and, of course in rural Cambridgeshire, rabbits and birds still made it into the pot. However, much Christmas food was 'mock' or 'fake', made to look like the real thing when it was far from the real thing. Some kind of meat with roast potatoes and roast parsnips was regarded as a real treat. Christmas puddings were virtually non-existent so jam roly-poly or a tart were often substituted, perhaps with some custard. Although milk was rationed no-one was going to notice if the odd pint here and there made its way to someone's Christmas table, or if they did, no one was going to complain. Out in the remote Cambridgeshire countryside it was doubtful anyone would even know.

Those who managed to invite an American GI to Christmas dinner fared a little better as the servicemen brought their own special parcel of Christmas provisions with them. Many tuned in to the radio for the Christmas broadcast by the king, but otherwise entertainment was home made. After lunch there might be a family walk, if the weather was suitable. Children played ball games or tag. In the evening board games, like snakes and ladders or ludo and non-gambling card games would be played, stories read or told by firelight or lamplight. Many more islolated homes did not have electricity and would be lit by a paraffin lamp, tilley lamp or candles. Carols would be sung, and, if anyone had a piano, there might be a musical evening or ceilidh with folk singing and dancing as someone played traditional tunes. In the more remote corners of Cambridgeshire celebrating Christmas in this manner did not end with the war and continued into the 1950s and 1960s.

Strikes, Struggles and the
Beginning of the End

This year was marked by a massive number of wartime strike actions. Nationally the unions had doubled their membership during the war and by 1944 almost half the national workforce was engaged in some type of war work. Industrial militancy had begun to rear its head once more but this time many of the protagonists were women and apprentices. The effect was dramatic. In 1940 the number of days lost through strike action was 940,000. Now there were over 2,000 strikes which involved the loss of nearly four million days working production. It was a staggering number and it could obviously not continue if Britain were to win the war. This large number of strikes only served to strengthen resentments – workers wanted a living wage and to maintain working standards.

Cambridgeshire was hardly affected as its main industry was agriculture and it made little difference to the city of Cambridge where the main livelihood was services to the university. However, members of the armed forces saw it as unpatriotic and large numbers of the public felt that, with the tide of fortune beginning to turn in favour of the Allies, every possible effort should be made to bring this huge, frightening and destructive war to an end.

Churchill was furious and reacted angrily by imposing Defence Regulation 1AA making incitement to strike illegal. In this he was actually supported by the TUC who felt that some of their members had gone too far and were holding the country to ransom, seeing the threat of crippling essential production by withholding their labour as a form of blackmail. Early in the war there had been many genuine grievances, but the TUC felt that the concessions granted had gone to the heads of a few and that all negotiations for wages and better conditions should now wait until the war was over. With all the signs that the tide was definitely turning, growing numbers of people from all walks of life felt that 'all hands on deck' should be the order of the day.

Improving Education

The Education Minister, R.A. Butler was charged with steering the Education Act 1944 through Parliament. There had long been concern over access to education for children from the working classes and poorer sections of society, particularly in the northern cities, and people were more aware than ever that a decent education system for every child would be essential for future generations to cope with an increasingly complex and mechanised world. It was also recognised that girls would have to be included in this plan. Females had demonstrated in both world wars that they were just as capable as men of working at different jobs and contributing to society, and that they could no longer be relegated to the kitchen hearth or the nursery.

This new innovative legislation would provide more time at school and free secondary education for all children without all the hidden costs and inequalities that would affect poorer children. Under the Act, Local Education Authorities (LEAs) were required to submit proposals for the reorganisation of secondary education into three main categories: grammar, secondary and technical, as recommended by Sir William Spens' report in 1938. Allocation to a particular category would be by means of an examination taken at 11-years-old which would be subsequently known as the 11+ exam. The intention was to provide equal opportunities for all children through a tri-partite system of education.

There would always be differentials in the potential of children. Some would be more academically inclined while others were more practically minded. Most parents who could not afford to let all their children stay at school usually favoured boys over girls because there were far more opportunities available for boys and because of the frequently mistaken notion that most girls' ambitions

Evacuee children, Cambridge Market 1944. (Courtesy of Cambridge Local Studies)

were simply to marry and have children. The school leaving age was also raised to 15 with a recommendation that it should be raised to 16 after the war.

Juvenile delinquency had remained a problem, although not so much in rural areas of Cambridgeshire as within the city of Cambridge, and the government now required all young people over 16 to register and offered them an increasing number of options including clubs and organisations which they could join and take part in activities. In rural Cambridgeshire, as in other rural areas, transport to these resources was going to be a problem, especially with petrol rationing in force. The usual reasons given for delinquency included absent fathers, working mothers, lax discipline and watching the wrong kind of films; but young people have rebelled against their elders since time immemorial. However, in wartime, vandalism was just an expensive and unwanted nuisance. It was essential that the enemy was not inadvertently given a helping hand by youths being stupid. Besides, the importance of the young replacement generation had long been recognised and there was great incentive to ensure that they were well trained and well educated to cope with the demands of an increasingly difficult world.

Cambridge University was extremely interested and concerned with proposed educational developments, and great attention was devoted to various committee reports on education which accompanied the 1944 Education Act. There was a growing problem which the university needed to address in that its numbers of graduate staff had outstripped the accommodation capacity of the university. There was also additional pressure to accommodate research students and it was suggested that a graduate college might be the answer. Fresh problems were created by the decision post-war to continue compulsory military service which affected the number of undergraduate entries. All men over the age of 18 would be required to do two years 'national service' in one of the armed forces, and this would also affect the age as well as the number of undergraduate entries. It was generally acknowledged in academic circles that the time for re-thinking and revision of the university's aims and objectives had arrived.

Accident at RAF Duxford

Out in the county, RAF Duxford suffered a dreadful accident on 19 July. The 78th Fighter Group based there had had a successful sortie against the enemy in the morning, although they had lost one of their best pilots during the mission. Soon after lunch a visiting B-17 Flying Fortress from the 95th Bomb Group landed. The captain, a friend of one of the pilots in the 78th Group, offered some of the men a 'ride around the airfield' in the B-17. Eight Duxford men eagerly joined the bomber's crew of four and its captain. The aircraft took off but failed to gain sufficient height quickly. As a result, the B-17, according to one report *'careered off a neon beacon on top of one of the hangars; lost its wing which crashed in front of the officers' club; dropped one of its rubber auxiliary tanks through an empty Nissen hut; and then crashed into the barracks of the 83rd where it burned, killing all on board and one man in the barracks. The barracks were completely demolished and all aboard the plane were burned beyond recognition...'*

The heat was so intense that even metal 'dog tags' (ID discs) were melted. The shock and grief felt by survivors was tremendous and there were numerous heartfelt tributes. On 22 July the funerals of the fourteen who died took place at Cambridge Military Cemetery, former comrades of the dead men following the long line of Union Jack draped coffins in respectful and sorrowful silence.

Meanwhile RAF Fowlmere had now been given over to the USAAF and assigned as USAAF Station 378, then allocated to the Eighth Air Force Fighter Command. It was said that, while Duxford was known to American airmen as the 'duck pond', Fowlmere was known as the 'hen puddle'. This is a good linguistic approximation of the names but also possibly alludes to the nature of the ground

King George VI and Queen Elizabeth talk to air crew, Cambridgeshire 1944. (Courtesy of Cambridge Local Studies)

in 1943 and 1944. Heavy rains soon caused problems on flat terrain that is good soft soil rather than hard bedrock. Station units allocated to USAAF Fowlmere included all the usual support facilities:

314th Service Group
467th Service Squadron
HHS 314th Service Group
331st Service Group
464th and 465th Service Squadrons
HHS 331st Service Group
18th Weather Squadron
72nd Station Complement Squadron
861st Engineer Aviation Battalion
1178th Quartermaster Company
1786th Ordinance and Supply Maintenance Company
989th Military Police Company
2120th Engineer Fire Fighting Platoon

In early April the 339th Fighter Group arrived from California commanded by the 66th Fighter Wing of the VIII Fighter Command. There were three squadrons: the 503rd, the 504th and the 505th Fighter Squadrons. The squadrons mainly flew on escort missions, but they would strafe enemy airfields or dive bomb enemy military units and marshalling yards if the opportunities arose. The squadrons were also active over the Channel and Normandy for the D-Day invasion.

Top Secret Meetings

Trinity College, with the statue of its founder, Henry VIII, standing in his favourite 'legs akimbo' pose, adorning a niche over the top of the entrance gate, above the arms of Edward III and his sons (who included the Black Prince and John of Gaunt), became a venue for top secret government meetings in 1944. These meetings were so secret it remains difficult to research or identify their purpose, or the nature of the subject/s which may still not be fully publicly available. There are three term lengths for embargoing sensitive information: 50 years, 70 years and 100 years. A great deal of information concerning the Second World War was released around 1995, 50 years after the end of the war. A fair amount of information has also been released during the first few years of the twenty-first century. The next major release date is now likely to be in 2045. However,

Trinity College Cambridge where secret meetings about D-Day took place in 1944.

educated guesses can be made and there are three or four possible events which occurred in 1944 that may well have been urgently discussed at Trinity in top secrecy. The first was Exercise Tiger, a rehearsal for the D-Day invasion, which went horribly wrong in Lyme Bay off the Dorset coast on 28 April and resulted in the loss of over 800 American troops and three huge tank warships. The news blackout was so complete that relatives of those killed were not told how or where they had died, even after the end of the war.

The second event was the actual D-Day landings in Normandy in June. In the early autumn Operation Market Garden took place 17-25 September and was an Allied attempt to liberate the Dutch cities of Eindhoven and Nijmegen by attacking Arnhem. Those who took part in these top-secret meetings may also have discussed the landing in Britain of the first V-1 flying bomb, or 'doodlebug' as it was known, on 13 June, followed by its even deadlier successor, the V-2, on 8 September, as well as the failed attempt by some senior German officers on 20 July to assassinate Hitler by planting a bomb in a briefcase in a room where he was due to hold a meeting. Hitler survived unscathed, but his trousers were shredded.

The proposed D-Day invasion of Normandy landings (code named Operation Neptune and the largest invasion by sea in history) began on 6 June 1944. It was the prelude to Operation Overlord which would begin the liberation of the German occupied territories in North-West Europe. In Britain, desertions from the Army increased, perhaps encouraged by memories of Dunkerque. However, there was great mobilisation of the armed forces at this time. Utmost secrecy about the D-Day campaign was paramount in order to take the Germans by surprise and proved to be very successful. Although the D-Day campaign took longer than had been expected, the operation was a victory for the Allies and the beginning of the end for the Germans.

Vengeance Weapons

However, the summer of 1944 brought a fresh menace from the skies. This was the V1 rocket, the 'buzz bomb' or 'doodlebug' as it was nicknamed because of the buzzing sound that was one of its chief characteristics. It was a monoplane which had no pilot. The fuselage was manufactured from welded sheet steel and the wings were made of plywood and its Argus AS 104 pulse-jet engine pulsed 50 times per second which is what produced the dreaded buzzing sound. The V1s were either ground-launched, using an aircraft catapult, or air-launched from a bomber. They were unable to take off independently due to the low engine thrust and problems with the small wings.

Code-named Cherry Stone, the V stood for Vengeance weapon (*Vergeltungswaffen*) but it initially had a limited range (150 miles or 240km) and most were fired at London or on Southern England. The missile was pre-set to trigger the arming of its warhead after about 37 miles (60km) and when the detonating bolts were fired, the VI went into a steep dive which caused the engine to stop. The sudden silence alerted those below that impact was imminent. London was a prime target for doodlebug attacks, but a number were also launched against Cambridge, although none hit the city, coming down instead in various parts of the county. One fell close to Mepal airfield near Ely on 29 September. Others fell at Melbourn, Burwell, Castle Camps, West Wicken and Heydon.

The V2 was an even more terrifying 'vengeance weapon'. It was, in effect, a long-range guided ballistic missile and it was manufactured to attack Allied towns and cities in retaliation for the Allied bombings of German cities. These missiles travelled faster than the speed of sound and rose as high as 50 miles above the ground when fired, sometimes destroying themselves on re-entry into the atmosphere. They could create a crater 66ft (20m) wide and 26ft (8m) deep and were capable of ejecting 3,000 tons of explosive materials. The first V2 attack was in September 1944. The speed and trajectories of these missiles made it almost impossible for them to be intercepted by fighter planes or anti-aircraft guns, and there was no guidance system which could be jammed. On 10 November a V2 rocket crashed near Fleam Dyke Pumping Station close to Fulbourn, destroying the railway bridge by Dullingham station.

Although the tide of the war was turning, there were a number of incidents involving more conventional aircraft in the county, some of which also involved USAAF planes and personnel. On the night of 18 April, Lancaster LL667 was returning from a mission to bomb railway marshalling yards in Rouen and reached Witchford at about 2am. As it came into land the plane was shot down by a Luftwaffe intruder and crashed in a field by the side of West Fen Road. The crew of seven were killed. Two of them, an English wireless operator from Yorkshire and an American bomb aimer from Connecticut, were buried in Cambridge City Cemetery. Half an hour after the crash Lancaster LL867, from the same 115 Squadron, was shot down nearby by another Luftwaffe intruder. None of the second plane's crew survived either and again two of them were buried in Cambridge.

There are over 1,000 graves in Cambridge City Cemetery for members of the armed forces, mostly British and Commonwealth members of the RAF. The incumbents may be strangers to both the city and the county, but simply had the misfortune to die in the area, most of them killed in air combat and plane crashes. Today the graves are maintained by the Commonwealth War Graves Commission and complement similar cemeteries throughout the country.

The Wonders of Dehydration

Food, both quality and quantity, was still high on the agenda. The government had now decided that the quality of strawberry and raspberry jam needed to be improved. In addition, apricot pulp had been purchased and brought in from Spain to make apricot jam. The women of Cambridgeshire shrugged their shoulders for the most part. Blackberries and elderberries were to be found in abundance in the local hedgerows, wild raspberries grew on the edges of the fenlands. Gooseberries, red, white and black currants could still be found on farms and in cottage gardens. Rosehips grew in abundance and herbs like mint and parsley were common. Many Cambridgeshire women simply jammed, jellied, pickled and preserved whatever was available. Blackberry, gooseberry and blackcurrant jams were popular and so too were mint jelly and redcurrant jelly. Tomatoes (with apples when they could be found) were made into chutneys. Small onions were pickled.

The 'wonders of dehydration' were discussed by Parliament. What this basically meant was the drying of vegetables which could be reconstituted as needed but would take up much less storage and carriage. The Minister of Food quoted the case of 1,000 tons of cabbage dried and reduced to 40 tons. He then went on to enthusiastically describe a new product: *'mashed potato powder, which was contained in a tin much like cocoa powder…one took a few teaspoons, poured hot water on it and got a very good mashed potato without any cooking in the home…I do not think anyone would know that it was not ordinary mashed potato.'* To the generation which grew up on 'Smash' this statement might raise a few wry smiles.

However, dried foods lose some of their nutritional value in the dehydration process and this fact had to be considered against possible savings in tonnage. Cabbage, which has become a rather despised vegetable in recent years, was highly recommended as an excellent source of Vitamin C. The body cannot store Vitamin C, which is essential to fight infections and maintain health, and ideally needs a daily dose. Fresh carrots were high on the agenda since they were in plentiful supply and a good source of Vitamins A, D and B12. Sprouts, now mainly eaten at Christmastime, but a traditional British winter vegetable, have a very high Vitamin C content and are also a source of iron as well as Vitamins A and B6. Dehydration destroys Vitamins A and C, and other elements, so the benefits of dehydration were a double-edged sword. While it reduced bulk, it destroyed the essential vitamins and trace elements necessary for health, but the troops needed every bit of energy they could muster from rations, and hard-working traditional Cambridgeshire farmers, who grew their own potatoes and cabbages anyway, were not going to eat powdered replacements which had none of the bite or fibre of the freshly cooked items.

Wartime school recipe books and home cooking in Cambridgeshire, as in many other counties, featured cheese and egg dishes, vegetable hotpots, stews and tarts, simple puddings, oat-based biscuits, as well as the ubiquitous rabbit stew and jugged hare. However, the Ministry of Food seemed to have learned a lesson from the last war in not promoting almost inedible dishes such as fried porridge scones or a brown puree replacement for vegetables made from stale bread and old vegetable leaves.

Hopes had faded that the war would be over by Christmas, but the tide of the war had turned and there were new initiatives on both the battle fronts and home front. The YMCA had instigated a scheme whereby they would deliver Christmas gifts to the relatives of those serving abroad. The British War Relief Society (BWRS) also paid for Christmas cards, savings stamps and gifts for children this Christmas. The BWRS co-ordinated charities in the United States which had raised funding to provide the British with clothes, food and non-military aid. The black-out was reduced as the threat from German bombers was now practically non-existent, and churches were allowed to light up their windows for Christmas. Cambridgeshire responded with some enthusiasm. They felt as though they had lived in the darkness for too long. The Ministry of Food allowed extra meat, sugar and sweet rations as a Yuletide treat.

In keeping with the tradition of reading stories, especially ghost stories, by candle light or firelight on Christmas Eve, Tim Munby, the librarian of King's College from 1947-1974, wrote a ghost story which was published for Christmas 1944. 'The Four Poster' is about a haunted eighteenth-century bed in which someone had died and whose original curtains had been used as the shroud for a dead convict. The bed retains something of 'a malign influence' and everyone who sleeps in it suffers dreadful nightmares and the risk of death themselves. Told around the fireside late at night it caused a number of folk to have their own nightmares. In addition, the Luftwaffe decided to add to the stuff of nightmares by choosing Christmas Eve to launch a fleet of thirty doodlebugs aimed at attacking the northern part of the country from Derby to Durham. It was the third anniversary of the Blitz on northern cities and a sharp reminder that the war was not over yet.

The Horrors of War Revealed

January 1945 was noted for its *'hard frost, considerable snow, and heavy rain with severe gales mid-month...'* In early February there was a fatal air collision over the village of Prickwillow. The aptly named plane 'Miss Fortune' (B-17G 43-37806) flew too close to another aircraft (B-17G 43-37894 from the 849th Bomb Squadron) and both planes locked wings. 'Miss Fortune' crashed on to two cottages below killing one of its crew members, two civilians on the ground and seriously injuring three more. The tragedy was made even worse by the fact that one of the dead was an 18-month-old baby girl. The other plane crashed at Bracks Farm in Soham and also killed one crew member. The aircraft was carrying a full bomb load which exploded causing a huge indentation in the ground.

The bombing of Dresden by the RAF and the USAAF took place on 13-15 February. It was a savage and prolonged attack which, ultimately, was in revenge for the vicious ravages of the Blitz and a kind of turning point. The RAF sent 722 heavy bombers together with 527 from the USAAF and dropped nearly 4,000 tons of high explosive bombs and incendiary bombs on the city. This created a firestorm which destroyed the city centre and an estimated 25,000 lives were lost. Cambridgeshire people, who, so close to London and the coast, had been vulnerable to the German war machine for so long, remembered the inferno of the Blitz created by the Germans, not to mention the terrible destruction of cities like London, Liverpool, Manchester and Coventry during the Blitz, felt that the Germans were now getting a long overdue taste of their own medicine; but there were a number of citizens who shuddered at the huge loss of civilian lives, especially those of children. They recalled only too well how it felt to lose members of their own families. At the same time, they understood that it was the German military machine which had caused their sufferings, not the civilians of German cities, and they sympathised to some extent with how it felt to be bombed without mercy.

Two further USAAF raids on Dresden followed which were aimed at destroying the city's railway yard and there was yet another one in April on the neighbouring industrial areas. In the seventy plus years since the bombing of Dresden claim and counter claim have been furiously argued. Was it necessary? Was it over-reaction? Was it just German propaganda which made it seem so bad? Was it an 'innocent city of culture' or a centre of munitions and armament manufacturing? Was it simply an attempt to scare the Germans into surrender? It was all and none of these things. To read accounts of the bombing of Cologne, Hamburg or Dresden, is dreadful; to read accounts of the Blitz on English cities is dreadful.

Isle of Man Air Crash

One of the strangest and saddest stories in Cambridgeshire connected with the war is the burial, at the American Cemetery in Madingley, of 31 victims from an air-crash in the Isle of Man. The accident happened about three weeks before the European war ended and still ranks as the Isle of Man's worst aviation disaster. The plane involved was a Boeing B-17G Flying Fortress belonging to the 54th Bombardment Squadron of the Eighth Air Force. On 23 April 1945 the aircraft was taking US ground crew and mechanics on a week's leave to Northern Ireland. The aircraft was flying at 500ft (150m) off the north east coast of the Isle of Man but had failed to take account of adjacent high ground and flew into the hillside of North Barrule 1.842ft (561m), a rugged hill of near mountain height in the

American Cemetery, 1940s.

north of the Island close to the village of Maughold. The plane exploded, killing everyone on board.

The Isle of Man is a Crown Dependency (reliant only for defence on Britain) and not subject to the laws of the United Kingdom. When the US commander from the plane's English base arrived, he was told that repatriation of the dead would be subject to the diplomatic rules of the Manx Government. Deciding that this would be simply too long and complicated a procedure, he ordered that the bodies should be flown back to England where they were ceremoniously interred in the American Cemetery at Madingley. Both Madingley and Maughold have commemorative plaques of the tragedy.

Victory in Europe and Japan

Hitler committed suicide on 30 April and the treaty of surrender was signed by the Germans a week later. VE Day or Victory in Europe Day was celebrated on 7 May by the Commonwealth countries, 8 May in Britain and Europe and 9 May in the Channel Islands. Cambridgeshire, especially the city and university, welcomed peace with a huge sigh of relief and many impromptu parties. People ran through the streets of Cambridge holding an effigy of the despised German dictator aloft to be burned on a bonfire in the manner of Guy Fawkes. There was sheer joy and exuberance that Germany was defeated, Hitler was dead and peace-time had come again. Lights shone once more in windows everywhere, Victory bonfires blazed, and the church bells rang out, but the war was not yet completely over. There was still the war with Japan.

Italian PoWs watching football. (Courtesy of Cambridge Local Studies)

In mid-March, almost two months before the European war ended, the government had realised that further call-up of military personnel would be required for the war against Japan which, at that point, showed no signs of ending. The army was now well equipped and well trained and new manpower would need time to be fully trained and assimilated, besides which it was recognised that the process of redeployment against Japan would be a complicated and difficult process. The Allies had remained at war with Japan and the Japanese government refused to surrender to the Allied forces despite the call for total Japanese surrender at the Potsdam Conference on 27 July. Invasion was considered but finally rejected in favour of using the so far untested atomic bomb.

On 6 August the first atomic bomb was dropped on Hiroshima killing 66,000 of its 255,000 citizens and injuring another 69,000, according to American figures. The Japanese still refused to surrender so Russia declared war on Japan and invaded Manchuria on 8 August, but the US had lost patience. The following day Nagasaki was bombed. Out of a population of 195,000 there were 39,000 dead and 25,000 injured, again according to American figures. Absolute figures are difficult to assess. Atomic explosions create firestorms which can cover several miles, incinerating everything in their path, and radiation sickness can kill many years after the event. By this time there was a division between the Japanese military who wanted to continue the fight and Japanese civilians who simply wanted an end to the nightmare bombing and to live in peace. The Japanese Emperor, Hirohito, whom many Japanese regarded as divine, had never really been in favour of the war but he had had little choice except to go along with it. After the bombing of Nagasaki, it was Emperor Hirohito who finally insisted that the war should end. Five days later Japan surrendered to the Allies and 14 August was designated V-J (Victory in Japan) day.

Shortly after the capitulation of the Japanese and the celebration of V-J Day (15 August 1945) the United Nations was established, and its charter ratified on 24 October. Britain was one of the five security council members and had a power of veto on decisions. The war against the Japanese on the Eastern Front, fought mainly in Singapore and Burma, has been called the forgotten war, although the troops involved endured some of the worst conditions. In addition to a ruthless human enemy the troops also had to deal with a great deal of hostile terrain, a fair-sized number of snakes and crocodiles, and tropical diseases such as malaria. Those unlucky enough to be captured were put on near-starvation rations, made to work long hard hours on enemy projects, the most famous of which is probably the Burma railway and the famous bridge over the River Kwai, and they were often made to stand for hours in water infested with reptiles.

It was the Cambridge Regiment's greatest misfortune that both battalions of the 'Fen Tigers' had to fight in Singapore and Malaya and that both battalions had to subsequently surrender to the Japanese. They paid a heavy price: 24 officers and 760 other ranks were either killed or died in Japanese captivity. For those who did survive it was a life changing experience, full of so many bitter memories, that most could never bring themselves to speak of it.

Wartime rationing would remain for some years and even increased in the case of certain commodities. To the astonishment of Cambridgeshire residents, allowances of meat, bacon, cooking fat and soap were further reduced only two weeks after VE Day. Meat rationing was made more severe by a transport and dock strike in mid-1947 causing thousands of tons of imported meat to rot in the containers. On 1 June a basic civilian petrol ration was restored, but even three years later, the petrol ration was only a third of what it had been at the start of the war.

Anyone who had hoped for a break after the war had ended, also found that the railways were sadly depleted. During the war freight and military requirements had been primary factors. Rolling stock was ageing and a considerable amount of it had been damaged by enemy action. Train services were curtailed and running times uncertain. In July parcels containing gifts of food which weighed over 5lbs (2.3kg) were deducted from the recipient's food rations in order to preserve fairness in rationing. Heavy summer rains in 1946 ruined the country's wheat harvest and bread was rationed. However, on

Survivors of Ely Company, returning to Ely 1945. (Courtesy of Cambridge Local Studies)

16 June the Family Allowances Act was passed awarding mothers a tax-free cash payment for each child. It was the first time in Britain that a payment from the State had been given directly to women.

Horrors of the Holocaust Revealed

There was yet another dreadful post-war shock in store for everyone in Britain, but especially for Cambridge and Cambridgeshire, both of which had been so heavily involved with the *Kindertransport*. Liberating forces in Germany and Poland had stumbled across possibly the most appalling war crime of all time. Soldiers were unable to believe the sights which greeted them when they reached concentration camps like Auschwitz, Bergen-Belsen and Treblinka. There were dozens of such camps across Germany and Poland but these three had acquired a reputation for unrivalled savagery towards their inmates. People, little more than bags of bones in the infamous blue and white striped utility clothing used by these establishments, clung to barriers to try and stand upright. Their Nazi gaolers had been brutal to the last. The 'lucky ones', if they could be called that, were at least still alive. They had survived the brutality, the beatings, the abuse, the rapes and the medical experiments, but at a terrible personal cost. Allied soldiers had tears in their eyes as they gazed at these skeletal scraps of humanity clinging to the wire fences and gave them whatever provisions they could.

The full horror of what had happened emerged slowly from piecing together the prisoners' stories, interrogating captured Nazi guards, and discovering at least some of the records which the Germans had tried to destroy. Day after day trains had arrived at these camps with their human cargo loaded into cattle trucks. The trucks were unloaded, the inmates rapidly sorted into groups. After the briefest of medical examinations, pretty girls, musicians and exceptionally fit-looking young men were selected for survival, but it was only a comparative few who were spared. The rest were then dispatched to the reception huts. Here they were ordered to undress completely and to remove any personal effects. Told that they were going to have showers before the distribution of clothing and personal effects, they were then herded like cattle towards the buildings where their lives would be ended prematurely in complete and utter degradation. Packed into huge chambers, the doors were then slammed shut and locked. Keen to preserve illusions until the last to prevent panic and opposition, the chambers had the appearance of massive showers. However, it was not water which was pumped into the chambers but a lethal toxic gas which choked, burned and asphyxiated the victims.

Second World War memorial at Trumpington.

In Cambridgeshire those who had worked so hard to enable children of the *Kindertransport* to be brought to safety were traumatised. Both city and county had subsequently sheltered and protected numbers of Austrian and German Jewish children throughout the war. How were they ever going to find the words to tell them what had happened to the family and friends they had left behind in their homelands, and that they would never be able to go home again. How could they ever begin to explain to them? How could this be allowed to happen? Who knew? Were all Germans intrinsically evil? Some British propaganda suggested that this was the case and that concentration camps would not have happened in France or Britain. However, there was a concentration camp on Alderney in the Channel Islands for most of the war. The inmates were mainly Russians, whom the Germans hated and one Russian who tried to escape was crucified on the camp gates as a warning against further attempts at escape.

The answer to who knew about these camps was simply that many ordinary Germans didn't know anything about them until after the war was over, and when they did, most were as shocked as anyone else. Hitler, the SS and the Nazi High Command had insisted on absolute secrecy over such matters and they had complete control of the news outlets. They did not want these activities known and anyone who raised questions often just disappeared. Hitler had been anxious to promote a vision of the good life under the Nazis, hence his insistence on the 'model occupation' of the Channel Islands, and now, along with everyone else, Channel Island evacuees would have to learn the terrible truth.

Epilogue

The Second World War is not usually regarded as such a bloody affair as the First World War, although far more people were killed in this war. The casualty toll in the 1914-18 war was around 38 million: 18 million deaths and 20 million wounded. The figures for World War Two were assessed at around 60 million deaths which equalled about 3 per cent of the total world population of that time. It is more difficult to be accurate about the numbers in this war because many bodies were incinerated without trace as a result of the bombing campaigns and especially the firestorms created by the atomic bombs dropped on Japan. Besides, in the First World War there were no deliberate attempts at ethnic cleansing.

There were fears in Britain that there would be a great deal of psychological damage caused by the scale of ethnic cleansing and the sheer destruction, so a number of clinics were opened to deal with problems but they were not needed and closed again fairly quickly. Some people suffered from panic attacks and disturbed sleep, which were natural reactions to what they had been through, some had serious problems, especially those who had been sent to death camps or captured by the Japanese, but it was a small percentage of all those affected. Even the Germans were moved to remark on the British 'stoicism'.

The Luftwaffe, under the direction of Herman Göring, had initially been confident that they could destroy British morale through their continuous daytime and night time attacks in 1940-1941. It didn't happen. No matter how much punishment the Germans meted out the British got back on their feet and retaliated. As someone once said, *'those guys just would not lay down and die...'* It was as much the British attitude as the fire-power and the dog fights that defeated the Luftwaffe in battles which they had expected to win. The outcome of the Battle of Britain, when Britain stood alone, was a huge blow to Germans, and Hitler himself commented that he was unimpressed by the fact the Luftwaffe seemed to keep missing their intended targets of manufactories, roads, railways and airfields, blowing up civilians, churches, cricket pitches and fields of sprouts instead. However, the spirited fight back by the young RAF pilots led Hitler to believe the country was much stronger than it actually was, and had he invaded at that point the outcome of the war might have been very different. Churchill was right when he famously paid tribute to the RAF after the Battle of Britain, saying *'never in the field of human conflict has so much been owed by so many to so few...'* Although the RAF lost large numbers of planes, Britain was so highly mobilised during that period that the country was actually manufacturing and turning out more aircraft than the Germans. Cambridgeshire took its share of the national pride because of the number of RAF airbases in the county and the support which county folk had offered the RAF.

The Commonwealth War Graves Commission was originally founded in 1917 by Fabian Ware with the aim of commemorating all those who died in the service of their country in the First World War, and subsequently, in the Second World War, by a name on a memorial or on a grave headstone (uniform to avoid class distinction) although the actual body of the serviceman might be missing from the grave. The commemoration of those who died in the last war had tended more towards war memorials of some description, however, this time many town and village graveyards had begun to include these Commonwealth War Grave headstones in their burial grounds. The grave itself might sometimes be empty but commemoration had been provided in the same manner as for people who did not die as a result of the war. This was especially important for aircraft personnel who died in locations far from home when their plane crashed or was shot down or a parachute jump failed.

In France and Belgium there are hundreds of tiny cemeteries, some in the middle of fields far from any village, which were the sites of fiercely fought land battles and soldiers lay where they fell. Britain was never occupied so many of

Base of Second World War memorial, Trumpington.

the casualties were from aerial fighting and included British, Polish, Canadian, Australian, American, some French and even a few German individuals. Numerous bodies of servicemen were repatriated after the war, but equally many were never found, especially those who had died in naval battles or bombings. The neat, rectangular headstones, made from pale Portland stone or Hopton Wood stone, are of an even height, evenly placed, and easy to recognise. Each headstone displays a cross, unless the person it commemorates is not of the Christian faith, or of any faith at all, and either an emblem of their country or a badge of the regiment in which they served. The stone also shows the name, age, military rank, unit and date of death for that person. There are Commonwealth war graves and dedicated Commonwealth graveyards in a number of countries. In Britain, where there are Commonwealth war graves in a town or village cemetery, there is a plaque on the churchyard gate simply stating 'Commonwealth War Graves'. The sheer numbers of these graves begin to give some idea of the scale of human losses during the war. It also gives grieving loved ones somewhere to go where they can remember and feel close to those they have lost.

The American War Cemetery at Madingley is the only graveyard dedicated to American troops in Britain and the only permanent American military Second World War cemetery in Britain. Many of those buried or commemorated here were members of the United States Air Force, who died helping the aerial fight against Germany, and the United States Navy who helped to gain ascendancy over the seas and who kept the supply routes open. It has 3,812 graves with another 5,127 names engraved on the Wall of the Missing. The neat rows of white marble cross-shaped headstones, arranged in the shape of the spokes in a wheel, the avenue to the memorial flanked on the south side by the Wall of the Missing, and the memorial building itself, are impressive. Eighty of the headstones are marked with the Star of David.

The Wall of the Missing, constructed of Portland stone, is 472 ft (144m) long, and four figures, each representing the American army, navy, air force and coastguard service, stand guard at intervals along the wall. The memorial, also built of Portland stone, has five pillars on its north face to represent the five years (1941-1945) that the United States was involved in the war. A message of tribute runs across the lintel above the pillars. Inside the memorial is a large room, with an enormous map showing American deployment and involvement in the Second World War and there is a small chapel at the far end. Despite the fact that the busy A1303 road runs along one side of the Cemetery, it is an incredibly quiet and peaceful place, surrounded by woodlands, with a feeling of great tranquillity. Glenn Miller (although his body was never found) and Joseph P. Kennedy (brother of President John F. Kennedy) are among those who have graves here, as well as the crew of the first American ship, the USS *Reuben James*, to be lost in the Battle of the Atlantic.

Despite the warm welcome given to the young Polish pilots during the war, and despite their heroic contributions to the battle for the skies, the British now made it very clear that they expected them to return to their homeland. A large number of Poles would have liked to return home, because the English weather, the English language and English cooking got many of them down, but Stalin still had a firm grip on Poland and many could not, or did not dare, return home. Numbers had been swelled by other Poles who had escaped the dual ravages of Hitler and Stalin. Both German and Russian armies had fought, plundered and raped their way across Poland and thousands had fled the onslaught. Many Poles settled in Cambridgeshire, Suffolk and Norfolk, places they had been introduced to when they first came to Britain, where their compatriots were stationed fighting the enemy, and where numbers of them would remain; although the longing for their homeland did not diminish and many grieved bitterly. Initially this situation brought forth grumbling, resentment and dislike among certain sections of the British population but some of these attitudes softened when the full extent of Stalin's atrocities and his infamous 'purges' became known, as well as Hitler's

Graves of American servicemen at the American Cemetery Madingley Road, Coton.

atrocities of the concentration camps and the Holocaust. However, in recent years this resentment has returned, continuing to fester, and has grown into aggression at what has been perceived as a great increase in numbers, although the Polish population still remains at around 1.7 per cent of the total population in England.

Most of the children from the *Kindertransport* who were evacuated to England in 1938-1939 never saw their parents again. The majority of the adults had been sent to the concentration camps and were killed by the Nazis in various horrific ways. If they escaped the fate of the gas chambers large numbers succumbed to overwork, starvation, disease, beatings, medical experiments etc. It was a horrific task for families, friends and foster parents to tell their young charges what had happened to their parents. Most of them tried to gloss over the details, simply telling the children that, sadly, their parents had died in the war. Those who had been very young when they arrived in Britain had little memory of their homeland or their parents, but those who had been either in their early teens, or on the cusp of their teens, and were now working, or serving in the British Forces, understood only too well what they were being told. They faced the full horror of what had happened and then many of them chose never to speak of it to their own children and grandchildren.

There was now absolutely no question that these *Kindertransport* children would, or could, ever return 'home'. Some had lost as many as twenty family members. Many were given British nationality. Some emigrated and received Canadian or Australian nationality. Those whose family were killed remembered the bravery of their parents in sending them to safety, knowing what their own fate was likely to be, and vowed to live good useful lives. Some parents did survive and came to find their children only to discover that they had formed new and lasting bonds with those who had cared for them during the war. There were many heart-breaking stories, but individual case histories are not included in this book to prevent possible future distress in the present political climate (2019).

Unexpectedly rationing hadn't stopped with victory for the Allies. Rationing would remain in force for some years and even increased in the case of certain commodities. Sweets were one of the last commodities to be de-rationed and that did not happen until 1953, eight years after peace had been declared. Cambridgeshire folk were amazed that bread would be rationed for two years until 1948. It had not been rationed at all during the war and this had raised hopes of being able to eat white bread once more. The hard winter of 1946/1947 ruined huge amounts of stored potatoes and so potatoes were rationed. Clothes rationing would finally end ended in May 1949, but the times of austerity were certainly far from over. For foods that weren't rationed the points system still remained.

Each person still had only twenty-four points to last them four weeks. Points were in addition to money paid for the goods, but it meant, for example, that no one could buy more than two large bars of toilet soap per month. This was aimed not only at rationing but also to deter hoarding and profiteering.

Some foods cost large numbers of points; others were not so bad. A pound (just under 500kg) of rice required 8 points; a tin of baked beans 2 points; a pound (just under 500g) of currants needed 16 points, while a tin of sardines only took 2 points. Families still had to plan carefully and needed to remember their ration books and their points allowances if they were away from home. Everyone was allowed 4 soap coupons for 4 weeks. A large tablet of toilet soap cost 2 coupons. Clothing coupons were also scarce. Each person was allowed 24 clothing coupons which might have to last up to a year. It was not an overly generous allowance as a man's overcoat required 16 coupons, a suit would cost 26 coupons, a pair of trousers needed 8 coupons and a pair of underpants 4 coupons. The ladies fared little better: a dress needed 7 coupons, a nightdress 6 points, a mackintosh 16 points and knickers 3 points a pair. Making the coupons last, or affording special clothes like a wedding dress, became a great skill. 'Make-do and mend' was still very much the order of the day. Coal, coke and paraffin supplies were also limited.

The slow repatriation of USAAF personnel began. Over two million American servicemen and women had been deployed to Britain during the war. Lasting friendships and relationships had been formed. Nationally there were as many as 70,000 GI brides who returned to America with their new husbands; but there was also the other side of the coin. Some GIs, who had wives, girlfriends, fiancées, in the States left broken hearts and illegitimate children behind which caused a good deal of grief. The shame of illegitimacy and the stigma of being a single mother in the 1940s were very strong and often scarred mothers and children for life. Cambridgeshire had its fair share of such cases, far more so than other counties which were not close to, or involved with, the USAAF airbases. There are still a number of those children alive today who know only that their father was American.

A few, using modern technology, attempted to track down their fathers but such efforts often end in heartbreak. One discovered, purely by chance, that his father was American, having been told that he had died during the war. Subsequent attempts to contact him resulted in complete rejection of the child, by now a young adult. The father had returned to the US unaware that he had fathered an English baby. He had married and had his own American family, and he was not keen to either explain or introduce a child he didn't know whom he regarded as an interloper. He simply did not want any kind of relationship. It was a story of heartbreak played out in a number of families, a consequence of war in a foreign land where a few moments of closeness might be all that a serviceman would ever have.

The withdrawal of the American forces also meant loss of business for companies and individuals where there had been large numbers of Americans stationed. Cambridge and Cambridgeshire noticed the loss of business from airfield personnel and the comparative free-spending of many GIs. A number of the RAF bases which were given over for the use of the USAAF did not survive and most of those that did decreased in size and purpose. The RAF took back control of RAF Duxford and RAF Bassingbourn late in 1945. RAF Bassingbourn was subsequently featured as the location for the '28th Bomb Group' in a 1950 Humphrey Bogart film *Chain Lightning* and it was also the airfield used in the film of *The Dambusters* made with Richard Todd and Michael Redgrave in 1955.

After the war RAF Bottisham was reclaimed and briefly used by Belgian airmen before closing in 1946, and today the site is almost untraceable. After the USAAF left RAF Fowlmere it was used by No.11 Group RAF Fighter Command for a short time, but it was closed in 1946 and was eventually sold by the RAF in 1957 for agricultural use. RAF Snailwell closed just after the war in 1945 and RAF Little Staughton was closed in 1947. RAF Oakington remained in use and was taken over by the army, the Royal Anglian Regiment being the last occupiers of the site. The runways at RAF Oakington were broken up after its final closure in 1999 and subsequently the 'hardcore' was used for the construction of the M11 motorway. RAF Duxford has survived as part of the Imperial War Museum group and is the largest aviation museum in Britain which includes reference resources, exhibitions, military vehicles, artillery and around 200 aircraft, as well as the Parachute Regiment and Royal Anglian Regiment museums. The Cambridgeshire Regiments have their own records and museum.

Ironically, Trinity College discovered shortly after the war that all the members of the infamous Cambridge spy ring: Kim Philby, Anthony Blunt, John Cairncross, Guy Burgess and Donald MacLean were all Trinity graduates. Recruited during the 1930s in Cambridge, they were mainly active during the Cold War which began in 1947, two years after the end of the Second World War, and didn't really end until the dissolution of the USSR in December 1991. The Cold War was essentially a political confrontation between the USSR (Russia), known as the Eastern Bloc, and the United States and its Allies, known as the Western Bloc. There was no armed warfare between the two sides but there was a great deal of dissension and diplomatic difficulties, as well as numerous political crises. Blunt, Burgess and Cairncross had also been members of the Cambridge Apostles, a small, exclusive, intellectual Cambridge student society.

After exposure of the spy ring, Philby, Burgess and Maclean fled to Russia. Cairncross and Blunt remained in England, but Blunt was stripped of his honours and his livelihood.

There was great excitement about the post-war election to be held on 5 July 1945. There had been a coalition government throughout the war and Churchill had received the necessary support from its Labour members. Labour Party members had pulled their weight on the Home Front; soldiers, sailors and airmen who held socialist principles had fought hard for their country and had given their all to defeat fascism every bit as much as Conservative members. Britain had been hailed as the most mobilised country in the war. Its women had thrown themselves into the war effort, ably supporting and assisting the men. This was supposedly the secret of its success and eventual victory. Furthermore, there had been no mention by the Conservatives of implementing anything contained in the Beveridge Report. Clement Attlee, the leader of the Labour Party, seized the moment, and he was quite unequivocal in his proposals for the future. Labour's manifesto (entitled 'Let Us Face the Future') contained proposals to nationalise the Bank of England, fuel and power, inland transport and iron and steel. Government intervention would be necessary, the party argued, to keep a check on raw materials, food prices and employment.

Following the Beveridge Report of 1942, the Labour Party had also formed plans to create a National Health Service and social security (BBC *The People's War*). Churchill, however, came out strongly against the Labour Party and its socialist aims and principles. *'I must tell you that a socialist policy is abhorrent to British ideas on freedom... a socialist state could not afford to suffer opposition – no socialist system can be established without a political police...* [a Labour government] *would have to fall back on some form of Gestapo...'* (Winston Churchill 1945). It was an extremely unfortunate choice of words linking a possible Labour government to the Gestapo, and, unsurprisingly, Labour won a landslide victory with an overall majority of 146.

Churchill was shocked, and he felt completely betrayed. He could not believe that he had led the British people successfully through the biggest war in history only to have them turn their backs on him. The facts were a little more prosaic. Churchill was an excellent wartime leader. That was his time. He was not a peacetime leader. His bulldog attitude, his impatience and his often harsh dismissal of issues and ideas, especially those concerning the working classes, were not suited to the changing society which was evolving after the war. This was Clement Attlee's time.

Clement Attlee had a passion for social justice ignited by his voluntary work in the East End of London before the First World War. The National Insurance

Act (1946) was passed, as promised, in that year, creating unemployment, sickness, maternity and pension benefits paid for by employees, employers and the government. True to Attlee's election pledges, the Bank of England was nationalised in 1946 and, on 1 January 1947, the British coal industry was also nationalised. There were still severe fuel shortages which meant that British Double Summer Time (BDST) was re-established for the summer of 1947. These were followed by the nationalisation of the railways in 1948 and of the iron and steel industries in 1950. The war had also finally forced Britain to realise that it was no longer viable to maintain a global empire and on 15 August 1947 India was granted its independence from Britain. Unable to find a solution acceptable to both Muslims and Hindus the country was partitioned into India and Pakistan which caused a number of problems that, 70 years later, have yet to be fully resolved.

Perhaps the most major post war innovation came on 5 July 1948 when the National Health Service (NHS) was established, spearheaded by the Minister of Health, Aneurin (Nye) Bevan. For the first time in history medical treatment was freely available to everyone. The NHS would become the envy of the world and a model for the future. Although the elite and entitled rigid class system, a love of bureaucracy, an innate distrust of foreigners, the hankering for an empire and national greatness which no longer existed, have managed to survive, the changes inaugurated by Clement Attlee's Labour government in the immediate post-war years changed the face of daily life in Britain forever.

Bibliography

The Story of Cambridge (Boyd, Stephanie. CUP)
WW2 People's War (BBC)
www.pastscape.org.uk
www.cambsaviationheritage.org.uk
Kindertransport archive (Churchill College Archive Department)
www.disused-stations.org.uk
Cambridge Central Library
Cambridge News and *Cambridge Independent Press* (Cambridge Central Library Local Studies)
American Cemetery and Memorial Madingley (American Battle Monuments Commission)
www.abmc.gov
https://aviationtrails.wordpress.com
www.kings.cam.ac.uk/archive-centre/
The Guardian newspaper
The Imperial War Museum Duxford
www.british-history.ac.uk

Index